NAVIGATING LIFE ANTHOLOGY

MINDSET, IDENTITY & RELATIONSHIPS

CLAUDINE REID MBE

Anthony

May God bless you
exceedingly, abundantly,
over all you can ask or
Even think. -Epu 3:20

Love from your
Sister - Claudine XXX

Love you, bro.

DIVINE
Flow
PUBLISHING

ISBN: 978-1-9196336-1-9

Layout and Publishing support Divine Flow Publishing Ltd, UK

Cover Design Marie Reid Chrispel Media, UK

Disclaimer:

This is a collection of stories by a diverse group of people. The views expressed are those held by each individual writer, and not necessarily those of Claudine Reid MBE or the other authors included in the collection.

PRAISE FOR NAVIGATING LIFE ANTHOLOGY
MINDSET, IDENTITY & RELATIONSHIPS

"Claudette openly shares how a lifetime of rejection and low self-esteem led her to settle for relationships that lacked love and where she suffered abuse from her partners; which consequently served to perpetuate the negative beliefs she had about herself. She gives a powerful account of her journey of transformation and how when we determine to submit to God's purpose for our life and commit to doing the work on ourselves; we can all truly experience healing and learn to love ourself. This is an honest and touching story that many will be able to relate to."

Julia Regis

"It's hard to believe and associate the word "shyness" with Rona Anderson. This lady is a powerhouse when it comes to motivation. I was moved all the way throughout Silence is Not Golden. Such a transformational and unique character who can show anybody that if they want to change the label of negative attachment they can! She is bold and she is enough. I truly applaud her for rewriting the label to unveil her true self and purpose."

Sherry Ann Dixon
Journalist and Public Speaker

"After reading Rona's section in this book about navigating shyness – Silence is not Golden. It amuses me how people make up their mind and are very quick to give labels based on their own viewpoint without giving the person much of a chance to shine or even the room to grow.

Sadly, when you are told something over and over – you begin to believe it. I can completely relate to Rona's experiences and I'm so glad I have the pleasure of knowing the real Rona and thankful she shared these experiences that affected her self esteem and the way she demonstrates her boldness in overcoming her doubts and fears. It's inspiring and a good lesson for all of us."

Helen Paul, Director
UGN Media Ltd, UGN Jamz Radio

"Sometimes we have to unbecome and remove the labels that we or others give us that are totally at odds with our authentic self.

Rona Anderson makes this clear in her contribution to this important anthology.

From Rona's opening paragraphs, it's obvious that she is an intelligent, bold woman who empowers others who took on board the label of being shy after she was told as a child that she should only speak when spoken to. This impacted every area of her life and meant she lost opportunities that would have helped her to grow professionally and personally.

Thank God we can unbecome and Rona shares how she did so.

Her journey to unbecoming is a powerful one and definitely worth reading if you want to change the label life has given you."

Marcia Dixon MBE
MD PUBLIC RELATIONS

"I recently read a quote that said, "A strong woman is one who feels deeply and loves fiercely. Her tears flow as abundantly as her laughter. A strong woman is both soft and powerful, she is both practical and spiritual."

I believe this describes Mother Thomas. She stood up for her faith and her family and was the first defender of the weak and the underdog. Like the Prophet Deborah in the book of Judges, Mother Thomas was an outstanding leader that served her church and community with courage, faith and humility."

Rev. Dr. Paul A. Hylton
Senior Pastor, Shiloh Christian Church
Middletown, Connecticut, USA

"This life story is evident of how God can turn someone's mess into a message.

No matter how dark or impossible the situation appears to be. There is a light (called Jesus) that shines at the end of the tunnel.

It shows that you can be a present day 'Shadrach, Meshach and Abednego'; someone who has been through the fire but doesn't look or smell like what you've been through."

Dr Ajoke Israel-Isiavwe
Co-overseer Kingdom Culture Movement
General Practitioner President Captivating Women

"Lilian's life is laid bare on the pages of this chapter. Whilst reading this, I felt I was walking the journey of Lilian's life with her. I love her love for her mother, her hopes and dreams as a child and into adulthood; her pain, fears and rejection by her father and the loss of her mother. Lilian's inner strength, resilience, tenacity and faith in God shines as does her journey to forgiving her father, uncle and relatives. This book is REAL and motivational, it will inspire you, make you laugh, fill you with joy and challenge you- to dream big dreams, aim higher, never to settle and importantly, how to forgive....to forgive and pray for those who have wronged you, hurt and harmed you. As Lilian says in this chapter "forgiveness has nothing to do with the other person, but everything to do with me freeing myself"

Gloria Saffrey-Powell BME

FOREWORD

This book is relatable and real! Books like this are few and far between, but are so needed today!

With many challenged with poor mental health, Navigating Life shows us how these women, from different walks of life, have overcome their personal battles.

I know for sure that there are women out there who have been through hard times, that they have swept them under the carpet. Normalising the abnormal, becoming immune or numb. These are situations that our minds and bodies have been through that have caused trauma, pushing us to act in a certain way or even behave as though it's a normal part of our lives.

When you read a book like this, and hear the stories of these women, it makes you realise you have also been through your own challenging seasons, and just how far you too have come!

You may be a person with a prominent title, or you may be a prominent figure in your family. Your family may say "you're such a strong person" but you know you have been hurt, you have confronted painful situations, you wore your poker face through it, but perhaps you felt at the time, you weren't sure if you were going to make it. But you will see, that if these women can make it, you can make it.

This book is for everyone! Men should read this book too! It will help men to understand not only the pain and wounds but also the strength of women.

I pray you enjoy this book, and the range of experiences shared within these pages helps you to understand, that people are the way they are because of what they have been through.

These women embody resilience and courage, and through their stories we can find hope.

Share this book. Tell people about it. It's going to save someone's life and help them realise they're not going through their challenges alone.

This book is truly life changing!

Lurine Cato MBE

MOBO Award Winning Gospel Singer

www.lurinecatomusic.com

CONTENTS

INTRODUCTION

Sometimes it feels like life has only dealt you with pain and heartaches. As you mature through these moments you learn to turn your pain into power.

Rejection, unforgiveness, shame and guilt. In this book, 16 valiant women uncover parts of their life journey. They show real and raw emotion to the sensitive hard issues of life.

These powerful stories take you on a journey of how, with fortitude, they were able to navigate a season in life when it felt like hope was gone.

The paradox is the muscle of resilience and strength is sometimes developed through the struggle, teaching us a plethora of lessons, whilst walking in the winter season and strain of the up-hill battle.

As you turn the pages of this Anthology analysing your own personal scars and remember that each scar is a reminder that you were stronger than what tried to take you out, each scar metaphorically says I survived.

The stories shared give hope and meaning to life - it serves as an encouragement to the reader, to let you know the key to your transformation and your next level of living starts in your mind. If you think you can or if you think you can't, either way, you are right.

As you navigate life remember, every season carries with it a new instruction, and every instruction requires something different from you. Stand in your strength!

My desire for every woman that reads this book is that she will see the beauty in the ashes of life, that she will find the courage, grit and clarity of thought in order to increase her capacity for more.

To your progress

Claudine Reid MBE

1

BE CAREFUL WHAT YOU LET YOURSELF BELIEVE: NAVIGATING REJECTION

DEBORAH GRANT

Sixteen years old and pregnant.

Her father, her rock is no longer around.

The father of her child is old enough to be her own father.

What does she do?

Who does she reach out to?

Mum is busy working to keep her and her younger sister fed.

Should she try to end the pregnancy?

Who would this child grow up to be?

Would it be a girl or a boy?

Healthy or not?

What?

These might have been the thoughts of my mother as she found herself pregnant with me by an old man. I was once told by someone close to her that she tried to abort me. I never asked her about it. I did not want her to confirm nor deny it. To me, the most important thing was that I am here.

You see, you must be careful what you let yourself believe. For many years, after that information was shared with me, I believed that I was unwanted by my mother. I grew up with a feeling of not being loved and not being worthy by the one person the world said I should have been. I believed the world until 2002, when my mother and her father reunited for the first time since she was a child.

The reunion was mind-blowing and revealing all at the same time. So many things made sense afterwards. My mother got her dad back. My mother's inability to love me the way I wanted to be loved was due to her yearning for her own father. It now made so much sense, but what did it mean for me?

My journey was only now beginning.

When you believe you are of no value and rejected, it can lead you into a constant state of trying to prove that you are worthy. I did just that. I sought knowledge because my father told me that was my escape and my way to independence. I pursued independence because, with independence, rejection would not be a possibility. Or so I thought. The more I was in control of my life through learning, I would not need anyone, and they would not be able to reject or hurt me.

It was this thinking that informed my every decision. I used rejection as a shot to motivate me to be better and prove them wrong, to make them sorry they rejected me. What I did not realize was that this approach was destructive. It destroyed my self-worth because nothing I did was ever good enough for me because I did not get the response I expected from them. I wanted affirmation. As much as I thought I was in control, I was covering up a part of me that never got a chance to develop, show up, and bloom because I worked it into submission.

I craved the kind of affirmation that feeds one's ego and self-worth that was being covered in busyness. I shifted my energy to helping others as another avenue of seeking self-worth. My primary environment for this was the church.

Church Life

The church was always seen as a haven where I could receive love. It is a place of acceptance where I would be celebrated and embraced, a place where I would feel I belonged because that is what the Word says. Well, that is what I kept hearing in Sunday school, so that is where I thought I belonged. This was where I would get to live my greatest life.

However, after many years, I realize that was far from reality. The church became a place of struggling to be seen and accepted. It seemed to be a place where you are used, and in some places, dare I say abused, especially as a single person—a single woman.

As a single woman, the natural nurturing part of you brings you into a place where you keep giving. And so often in my earlier days in church work, I remember giving to the point where I literally felt as though I was being scraped on the inside. I felt like being scraped emotionally because I had nothing more to give. There was no one there to say to me, *"You need to stop and fill up ever so often." "When you keep pouring into others, you need to keep pouring into yourself."* No one told me that. So, I just kept giving and giving and giving until that moment I felt so raw. I had to stop.

When I recognized the importance of filling up, that made a slight difference, but I continued to just fill up in order to give out again, as opposed to fill up and give out from my overflow. I was filling up just to pour out, and when I got empty again, it would be a vicious cycle of filling up to pour out. I found myself, in some cases, volunteering to be everything that I was asked to do or I saw that needed attention.

Because of my varied skill set, there was something that needed to be done every time, and I would volunteer to do it.

Eventually, I was just doing, doing, doing, and not being —not being in God's presence. Not being in the fullness of who I am as a person. I was just doing, and everyone was happy because someone else was doing it. It was not because they thought I was good or I had so much to give, but because since I was doing it, it meant that they did not have to do it. I did not realize that. I thought that I was such a good Christian girl and worker for God. That in doing these things, it would make me good. It would definitely show God how good I am for Him, but that was all false.

That is not what God wants from us, but that is what I gave. That was the way I saw it. What I was doing was trying to overcome my childhood—that feeling of abandonment, rejection, of not being enough, of unworthiness, and of low self-esteem.

People would say, *"How can you be saying that when you seemed so confident?"* But those were the trimmings and facades that were used. When we stop and go down into the deep crevices of our being, we'll recognize that we are just covering up what is really happening on the inside of us.

That was when I realized I was using work to medicate my pain. It is somewhat like an addiction. My bar was church. My addiction was church work and church ministry.

I had to stop and cry out to God, *"What is it? What is it that you want me to do? Who am I in You? Who do You want me to become? What is my purpose here because I know what I'm doing is not it? I know what I am doing is just putting on a show. I know that you know that it is a show. I need you to help me be of service to you and not put on a show for man. Not to put on the facade for man, but to be walking in your guidance and direction."*

That was the start of my journey towards discovering who I am in God, not who I am according to man's standards.

Relationships

As a single person within the church, not only was I abusing myself in terms of church work, but I also abused myself in terms of being a sensual being. I would see other people living what I saw as "happy lives". I wanted that for myself, so I nurtured friendships with Christian men, hoping that it would lead to dating and then marriage.

What I discovered was that some Christian men thought and behaved no differently to worldly men. I felt cheated; somehow, I bought into a lie that people in that environment were way different than those in the wider society, but they too just saw church as an opportunity to use and get what they wanted. It was not a case of really wanting to have that wholesome relationship that God intended.

I learned this lesson late in a relationship, but early enough to end the relationship and break any soul ties that had formed.

Now, I know my worth. I know exactly what or who I want to share my space with. Regardless of where you come from, whether the person is in the church or outside the church, I would not be so busy or caught up with everything else that I miss or allow myself to be used or be a convenience for anyone.

I now have boundaries, and I can say *"no thank you"* and move on if a friendship is not beneficial for me.

Church has often been likened to a hospital where sick people come in to be healed. As I go through my healing process, I am learning how to set healthy boundaries and build better relationships.

Rejection

How does the rejection issue play out? Life can turn into a checkbox exercise, and everything you do is measured on an invisible scorecard. But there was no constant degree of joy or peace. There was always the concept of "next" on the "to-do" list. I felt like life was in a holding pattern. I was never given the opportunity to truly immerse myself in the emotion of an experience. It was not allowed to happen because of the ever-present fear of rejection.

I was always in a place of bettering my last tasks and last achievement, all in the race for that ever-elusive "well done." Other elements of rejection raised its head. This time, it shows I was financially capable of being there. It proves my wardrobe was worthy of being there. It affirms that my hair was distinguished enough to be there. This all led me into another season of destructive behavior.

Change In The Narrative

About five years ago, I had a heart-to-heart conversation with God. I started asking Him some questions. I wondered why my relationships are not working out. Why am I always so busy? Why is there no one acknowledging the things I am doing? Why am I only seen when they are looking for someone to do a task? Why? Why? That powerful word was the beginning of the change in the story I was believing. It brought me first to a place of asking why I was doing what I was doing.

The "why", eventually took me back to childhood memories. The memories that had stories attached, but I never questioned their truth. The stories that were presented to me were filtered through a broken lens. I could not see the truth in its fractured state—a state that led to a life of unhealthy behavior. I had never questioned my behavior or thought of it as being influenced by anything other than the truth presented to me.

Now, I've started to reshape and retell my story. I determined that the characters had to be re-examined.

On the 16th of March 2021, I had "the conversation" with my mother. She was disturbed to know that I did not feel loved. She wanted to know why I believed this. What I discovered through her story is that she too had to be careful about what she believed.

It led us to the story of the person who told me that unloving bit of information around my birth. This story led her to share her own rejection, which showed up in her becoming withdrawn and protective of herself. It led her to look at her own journey of rejection in a different way—a rejection I received as her rejection of me.

The stories we believe have led us on a road of rejection exhibited in different ways. We are now on a journey of re-writing the stories we were both told. We are both now believing that these new stories can bring us to beautiful new memories—a new belief.

2

TRUSTING GOD: NAVIGATING AN UNCONVENTIONAL FAMILY

SHEVONNE CARVEY

My name is Kreea. I was born in the 80s, and my first few years of life was filled with constant love. I was surrounded by aunties, uncles, cousins, and grandparents that loved me dearly. Family was everything. With all that I experienced in life, it all began with love being my foundation.

From the age of 13, I had this feeling of being connected with God. I regularly attended church with my best friend at the time—the vibe, the energy, and the love I received felt just like home.

My Gran, who lived in Jamaica, heard that I'd started going to church and now a Christian. She was over the moon as she'd prayed hard for her family, and her prayers were answered. She sent me Bibles in abundance and regular scriptures when she wrote to me. I felt proud because she was proud that I was finally on the right path.

As I grew up, I drifted slightly from church but not from God. I could always feel Him close. My parents didn't go to church or practise any religion, from what I could see. When I would go to my nan's house (mum's mum) for the weekend, she would take me to church with her, and I would go to Sunday school which I always enjoyed.

Sadly, I witnessed domestic violence in my household. Seeing mum go through so much and not being able to help, say, or do anything really made me resentful towards her partner at the time. I just could not understand why mum wouldn't leave since all she did was cry and get mentally, emotionally, and physically abused any time alcohol was present. Whenever we would flee and move somewhere safe, she would always go back and bring him to our new house, which made no sense to my brain at that age. My escape, however, was going to my dad's every other weekend. At his house, there was peace and freedom from the shouting and domestic abuse. I did, however, feel sad for my mum and siblings. They had no escape from the toxic environment. I wished I could have brought them all with me.

I remember we moved three times to three different boroughs, and I ended up attending three different schools. When I turned 12 (year 7) in secondary school, our family finally settled—just me, mum, and my baby sister. It was peaceful, and I was able to do the whole of secondary school from years 7-11 without having to move —no disruptions, no changing of friends, just stability. What a beautiful experience it was, and I was very thankful to God.

Motherhood

While I was at college, I met someone a little older than I was who was loving and caring towards me, and we got into a relationship. Mum, dad, and all the family liked him, and I got on with his family.

Then at age 19, I became pregnant with my first child with my boyfriend. He had previously proposed to me about a year prior, and life felt perfect.

We both started attending church together and formed some lovely relationships with the people there. It was such a loving and welcoming environment. While there, we were advised about the importance of marriage, Bible teachings on 'no sex before marriage', and how much it honours God when we give our all to Him. Although my boyfriend and I were engaged, I can honestly say now that I was not ready for marriage.

By the time I was 20, I'd had my one-year old child. I didn't understand the concept of married life. Being engaged was fine, and we were in no hurry to go further. However, as a new believer, I wanted to be pleasing in God's eyes. I wanted to be accepted, so I opened my heart to learning and understanding marriage. We undertook pre-marital counselling every Saturday for six weeks, and I really did enjoy everything about it. I felt ready once the counselling session had run its course

Married Life

On November 5th, 2006, we got married in our church, then completed the legal logistics the next day. The blessing was beautiful, very overwhelming, and the love that was in that room was incredible. Everybody came out to show us love and support, and I felt ready for this new journey ahead.

Married life was different. Although we were young, there was a different level of respect given to us everywhere we went based on the fact that we were married.

In 2007, my husband and I welcomed our second child into our family. Life was great; I was happy, and my husband was working and happy, and we were raising our children in church. We were serving in the church, running the youth ministry, and I was also part of the worship team. I knew God was pleased. Everyone looked up to us at church and in our community. We were always hosting in our house because it was full of love, happiness, and a family with God right at the centre.

The Split

As the months went on, things began to change. My husband begun to slip into his old habits. He used to take drugs in his past, and as he slipped away from the path of God, he drew closer to his old path. He wasn't getting up early and praying anymore, and he wasn't meeting up with his Christian friends. Something happened within him that created this switch, and I wasn't sure what it was. In my opinion, nothing had changed between us to cause this sudden change. When I communicated with him, he reassured me that all was okay, but his actions said differently. It was scary.

Everyone around us believed that my life was perfect; they were unaware that I was going through so much inwardly. I felt like I couldn't really speak to anyone about it because it was "married people" stuff, so I kept everything to myself.

Over time, emotionally and mentally, I left the relationship before we actually split. I couldn't do this anymore. I cried and prayed in secret at night and smiled in public as if everything was absolutely fine. I prayed that this marriage would just end because it was too heavy to deal with alongside being a young mother. My faith had gone, and my vows began to fade.

One day, my prayer was answered. I was at home with the children and my husband. I went out to see my friend as I needed to get out and get some fresh air. It was a warm summer's day in June 2009. I took a brisk walk, breathing in the cool summer breeze and got in my car. I wound my windows down and turned the music up loud. I felt at peace, and at that moment, happy. I came home and noticed my husband looked different; something wasn't right. He came up to me and asked me where I was. I told him, and he said I was lying. At that point, he started following me around the house, so I began to walk away from him and the children. He followed me into the bedroom and began to question where I was. He got in my face, pushed me on the bed, covered my mouth, and had his hand round my neck to stop me from making a noise. I continued screaming, so he tried to put something in my mouth to quiet me.

In this moment, my strength began to slip away. I said a silent prayer to God and asked Him to save me and not let me die. I instantly got a dose of strength and began to fight him off me. I could see in his eyes that something wasn't right; they were extremely wide. I began kicking, scratching, and punching, and he got off and ran out of the house. I called my neighbours, and they took the children to their apartments and sat with me while I waited for my parents to arrive. The police were called, and it took me 45 minutes to calm down and make a statement.

After this event, my husband and I split. I was relieved because that chapter was finally over.

I cried because I was young with two children, and I didn't know how I would continue on my own. I thought about all these things I'd miss—the good times, surprise gifts, flowers, dates, his thoughtful side, and everybody coming over to our home. I was 24; I should be enjoying this time of my life, having fun with my husband, friends and family, being happy enjoying motherhood, but instead, I was unhappy and trapped.

Backslidden

Being with someone a little older than me made me grow up real fast. So, when I left my marriage, I got involved with someone younger than me who I had known growing up. He allowed me to re-live my youth exactly how I imagined it to be. I slipped away from church and stopped fellowshipping with my Christian friends. I felt a little let down by my church family. The support that was there when my husband and I were in the church doing ministry was gone. I looked around and felt like I was on my own on this journey. This made it easier to drink, party, and live what I thought was my best life, and at that moment, I enjoyed every minute.

My new relationship was fun. My children's father or soon-to-be ex-husband had set up a routine where he had the children on the weekends, allowing me some freedom. He was undertaking a programme where he was getting the help he needed for his addiction, which reassured me that they would be safe in his care.

He also met someone very lovely and family-oriented— the children loved her, and she had children of her own that our children got on with. I was really happy for them and his new family.

As the months went on, I began to see red flags in my new relationship, but I was so in love with what he looked like that I stayed in the relationship. He was tall, handsome, chiselled jawline, and had such a beautiful smile. He looked like a model and little did I know he'd done a few modelling jobs. On the outside, he was perfect, and I wasn't the only one who thought so, of course. He came with all the fans that also wanted him. He was younger than me and loved all the attention. I mean, who wouldn't?

Three years on, and I fell pregnant with my third child (my new partner's first). If anything, the baby had put much more pressure on the relationship and highlighted our pre-existing problems.

The relationship became toxic: arguments, mental and emotional abuse going both ways. It brought out a side of me that I didn't even know existed. I wanted to leave, but I didn't know how, and to be honest, deep down, I loved him so much (or the idea of him). I didn't want to lose him, but I couldn't explain why. Everybody around me could see that the relationship was unhealthy, including my parents, but an unknown pull kept me there. Any time I said I was done and meant it, something would bring us back together.

One day, I remember my second born saying, '*Mum, why do you keep letting him come back here if he makes you sad*'? That broke my heart, and I got an instant flashback of myself as a child looking at my mum and thinking the same thing. 'JUST LEAVE!' We all know as an adult, it is easier said than done. However, when your child can see things are wrong and speaks, you have to listen and act fast! I knew I didn't want history to repeat itself.

University

I needed a focus; I needed something for me. I was beginning to lose myself to this man, so I decided to enrol in a university. I had an interest in the brain and why people did what they did and thought the way they do. I began my degree in psychology and started going to a new church. I stayed around family and friends that continued, and they encouraged and reminded me of my worth.

University was going well; it was hard with a two-year old, but I stayed persistent and balanced my time. I didn't have time to entertain arguments with my boyfriend anymore, as all he did was break me down emotionally, and now, I was mentally on the rise. While I balanced university and motherhood, I began to get messages and calls from other females he was involved with. After having conversations with these women, something occurred to me; we were all hurting women in pain, reacting out of anger based on how we felt this man had treated us. We all wanted the same thing: THIS MAN, who we were allowing to disrespect us and turn on each other. It was time to refocus and stop entertaining back and forth conversations with these women and stop entertaining him. It was time to heal!

In July 2018, after failing a year and having to retake it, GRADUATION DAY FINALLY ARRIVED. I did it!!! Given all the obstacles presented, I did it. I was so proud of myself, and my parents were just as proud, maybe even more, of seeing their daughter's accomplishment. Seeing the smile on their face made it all worth it. My children were there and watched me go through so much—the late nights, sad days, neglect to meet deadlines, and so much more. Nevertheless, they got to witness mummy grace the graduation stage. They all got to see living proof that nothing in life comes easy, but you cannot give up.

I sat in my chair, and as I waited for my class to be called up to the stage, I began to reflect on the last couple of years. I said to God, "*I would never have made it without you. Thank you isn't even enough. I met some beautiful people in this university that became friends. Thank You, Father, that even though I lost myself, lost some friends, and a few church family members, I didn't lose my relationship with you.*"

It made me realise that even though I stepped away from God, His hands were and always will be on my life. I ran away from Him several times and ended up running into Him every single time. He always allowed me to go so far away from Him and do as I please before my plans crumbled. Then He will draw me right back into His arms. I was always reminded through it all that people will come, and some would go, but my relationship with my Heavenly Father was unconditional. He forgave me over and over again every single time I messed up. His grace was sufficient, so each day, I make sure I ask for forgiveness and thank Him for all that I have, as that's the very least I can do.

At Peace

Two months after I graduated, I was pregnant for Mr model. I know, I know. It was one weak moment I had, and that was it. He made it clear he was not interested, and I was on my own even though we already had a child together. I didn't know what to do; I just got my degree. I was working, my children were of a decent age where they weren't that dependent on me, and I was ready to go into my graduate job. I felt like all I'd done the past decade was have children (not that there was anything wrong with that), but I wanted to get my graduate job. I wanted to be married or be even in a relationship and do it God's way. I began to have thoughts of abortion. I felt like I'd taken ten steps back and was so disappointed with myself. One night, I had a dream, and my nan came to me in the dream and told me what I was having. I woke up and my decision was made. I was doing this, even if it meant alone.

Four beautiful children later, I am blessed and highly favoured. I have supportive and loving parents that have my back in everything I do. I have built an amazing relationship with my mother, which wasn't so strong growing up based on her decisions and how I viewed her. However, we discussed the past and allowed our relationship to be healed. We now have such a strong bond. My children's fathers are amazing, and they support me with the children. Through many honest discussions, we were able to come through all our past hurts and experiences and be the best parents for our children. Just like God forgives me, I have forgiven them for what they have done and asked them for forgiveness as I played my part, so I had to apologise for my wrongdoings. I have forgiven myself, which is so important to do. I have beautiful friends who are family like no other, and they always encourage me.

My children rise and call me blessed and always tell me how grateful they are to have a mother like me. My life isn't perfect, but I am so thankful and appreciative for my journey and all that God has in store for me. I am at peace with life and ready to elevate.

'The only limit in life is the one you put on yourself'.

3

A LEADERSHIP TALE: NAVIGATING LEADERSHIP

DR. CARMEN MCPHERSON

The morning started like any other. I got to work at approximately 5:45 a.m., a whole hour before anyone else was scheduled to be in the building. Apart from the head custodian (janitor) and his early morning shift crew who were scattered about the building, there were no other persons around. All was quiet. It was my favorite time of the day, just how I liked it. Me, myself, and I in the stillness. This time allowed me the headspace I needed to pray, gather my thoughts, review emails which were many, and set up materials, meeting agendas etc., for the day ahead.

I had spent the previous day, March 30th meeting, with different teacher groups. You see, as Principal (Headmistress) of one of the toughest schools in the State of Connecticut, a school which had secured a failing record for aeons and had at one point been dubbed a drop-out factory, leading in this environment was no ordinary feat.

The Backdrop

Starting in 2001, long before my arrival there, the school's credibility was first brought into question. The headlines of local media houses often chronicled the failing status of my school. Tantalizing news media headlines and articles, messy as they were made for salacious reading, were very much the norm. And although several Principals and Assistant Principals had all in their own way taken the necessary steps to address the ongoing concerns raised about the school, the negative press continued.

Monday, August 23, 2010

On day one of the 2010/11 school year, the Principal who had hired me as Assistant Principal at the school abruptly resigned. A private education management company had been given the task of turning the school around in two years with a $2.5 million federal grant. When I asked her who would run the school, seeing as she was resigning, my former Principal looked me square in the eye and said, *"You, until they find my replacement."* I told her she had to be kidding. She said, *"No, you can do it."* So, just like that, I was the Acting Principal for the first five weeks of the 2010/11 school year.

Monday, July 8, 2013

Fast forward three years to 2013, I was officially appointed as Principal of the School. By now, just as quickly as they had come, the much-celebrated private education management company's turnaround team and their plan had long gone. They left no lasting legacy or evidence of their presence at the school. No improvements whatsoever had been made. In fact, a 2013 newspaper headline had read, if you attended my school, the odds of you graduating were highly unlikely.

So, I began my leadership tenure in a school where the morale among the staff was one of school reform fatigue. A cynicism lingered in the atmosphere. There was nothing really left to show for the $2.5 million turn-around model that was implemented just three years earlier.

I, on the other hand, confident in my knowledge of the school, the staff, the students, the community, the history, and the overall environment, along with six years there as Assistant Principal under my belt, with a sense of optimism and hope, knew what needed to be done to move the school forward.

My school had had a long track record of media headlines and concerns around its failing academic status and safety issues. Students arrested after brawls in classrooms and hallways that disrupted the entire school were fodder for education journalists. They took pride in sensationalizing the effects of the inability of some of our students to cope with the stressors they faced. Our students lived on the side of town where gang activity was real, murder was commonplace, and many had either lost a peer, a friend or relative to gun violence or knew someone who had. Trauma was real.

Thursday, March 31, 2016

So, it was against this backdrop that my early arrival to work on March 31, 2016, took on significance. The purpose was to prep and fine-tune the last-minute details for the April 1st visit by the State's Education Department. They were coming to assess how effectively we (I) had managed the almost two hundred thousand dollars they had awarded us in school improvement grant funds for that academic year.

The work was continuous, but we had implemented, among other things, some academic and social-emotional supports for our students.

A martyr to the cause, I had chosen to take only five of my fifteen vacation days the previous summer. Who was I kidding? My ex-husband (no surprise) had continuously lamented that I cared more about the job than him and the relationship. He just did not understand, I'd reasoned. The summer we got married was the same season I assumed the role of Principal, but then that's a whole other story for another day.

So, back to the day in question, March 31, 2016. My agenda for the morning was going well. I had just finished the first set of meetings with the teacher leaders in the building and returned to my office when I received word from one of the neighboring middle schools that there had been a fight between some of their students and ours the evening before, and threats had been made. The boys who had fought were located and separated. I asked the Assistant Principal in charge of the boys to contact their parents and have them come and collect their children. All to ensure that the situation did not spill over into the day.

However, unbeknownst to me, the Assistant Principal had instead called for a school resource police officer, and the boys remained in school. I later saw the boys in the cafeteria and again asked parents to be called and the boys taken home. Oh, did I mention that prior to this, the day had hardly begun when a student was found incoherent in one of the stairwells and had to be taken to the hospital after ingesting an unknown substance?

Anyway, around 10:00 a.m., my secretary knocked on my office door to tell me that three students wanted to see me about an urgent matter. I took them into the conference room, and for the next forty-five minutes, the students revealed to me in detail how one of our long-term supply teachers had engaged in sexual intercourse, ongoing inappropriate conversations, and uncomfortable comments with at least two of them. They went on to reveal that there was at least one other student that the teacher had met on a website. The incidents were escalating, and it was not yet midday.

As the horrors of their story unfolded, I called the school's sexual harassment officer into the meeting for her to bear witness to what was being said and take statements from the children. I then went to call the school districts' Central Office. Unable to reach either my immediate supervisor or the Personnel Director, I took matters into my own hands. I knew what to do. I asked another Assistant Principal to find classroom coverage for the supply teacher in question. With a security guard in tow, I went to the classroom and asked the teacher to collect his personal belongings and come with me.

In my office, I let him know that some serious allegations of a sexual nature had been made against him, with evidence (the students had shown me text messages). At which point he went into denial, *"Who, me?" "No Miss, please don't tell the agency."* Now, who was he kidding? I informed him that the agency had already been notified, and with that, he was escorted out of the building.

The day was unravelling fast.

No sooner had the supply teacher been escorted out of the building, I was informed that an ambulance had been called to the school. The fighting boys' parents from the previous evening were never called and thus fought. One of the young men ended up being stabbed with a pencil. Needless to say, when the incident hit the news a couple of evenings later, the report would state that a student had been stabbed at my school! It did not matter that it was with a pencil; the fact is that a child had been stabbed. Such media reports were never good, and as Principal, I went into mental triage mode on viewing the newscast myself.

By 1:00 p.m., I was finally able to reach the Personnel Director to inform her of the supply teacher incident.

Then around 1:30 p.m., my immediate supervisor called to inquire about the stabbing. The Personnel Director had not shared the supply teacher information with her. While the stabbing was important, I proceeded to let my supervisor know that I had been trying to reach her about the sexual indiscretions.

As the day unfolded, I recall thinking how grateful I was that all these events were happening the day *before* the State Education Department's visit and not on the D-Day.

The type of incidents that occurred on that day would probably have taken place over the space of a year or two, maybe. But it seemed as though something was in the air, and a narrative had begun that would change the trajectory of my life in a major way. But for now, after filing reports with child welfare services, calling parents, filing police reports, and emailing all other needed summaries, some almost 16 hours after my arrival to school that morning, I left work that night at 9:00 p.m.

Friday, April 1, 2016

The following day, the State's Education Department consultants conducted their visit, met with the teachers, visited the classrooms, met with my immediate supervisor, and reviewed documents and data. We successfully ticked the requirements of the grant and were awarded the grant for the following year. That was a big win, yet I wasn't able to take it in fully. That afternoon, as I made my way home, I began plans to take three much-needed mental health days the following week. My body had begun yelling at me. I had awakened at 1:00 a.m. that morning with crippling muscle spasms in both legs, spasms that held me in a vice-like pain I had never experienced before and have yet to experience again. My friend, a registered nurse, warned me that I needed to go to the doctor that day, April 1st, instead of going to work. I couldn't follow her command, for as you the reader already know, I had an important visit scheduled.

Saturday, April 2, 2016

Meanwhile, as the weekend progressed, there was a flurry of activity as the events of March 31st began to take on a life of their own. Emails started trooping in from all corners. The teacher union rep in the building wanted to know what statement would be made to the teachers about the supply teacher. One Assistant Principal in earnest was insisting that child welfare services needed to be called. I kindly reminded him that all the necessary steps and protocols had been followed. By now, I had long been used to the subtle and at times, not-so-subtle undermining of my leadership and actions. So, I was not in the least taken aback by the second-guessing that was occurring. Still, as I cc'd my immediate supervisor on my replies to these emails, I asked her how best to respond to all the questions. *"Let them know it is a personnel matter"*, she had said, and that was that.

Monday, April 4, 2016

Five days later, at approximately 9:53 p.m. that night, I received an email from the Director of Human Resources. My presence was requested at a meeting in her office on the following day at 11:30 a.m. I read that I had a right to Union Representation. My immediate supervisor, a series of other directors, and the president of my union, were all copied on the email. As if knowing the writing that was forming or perhaps had already formed, I texted my supervisor and asked her point blank if I was being placed on leave. Her reply was, she did not know.

April 5, 2016

On entering the meeting room and sitting, I was immediately handed a letter by the Personnel Director and told that I was being placed on paid administrative leave from my position as Principal due to 'serious concerns' at my school. I was further told that Human Resources would carry out an investigation. When asked by my union representative the nature of the concerns and who would conduct the investigation, the Personnel Director cited the supply teacher's actions and a fight that involved a student being stabbed as the main concerns. She went on to state that they would be 'looking into a number of things.' I was informed that I was not to enter the school or have any contact with students, parents, or staff at the school. The leave was effective immediately. Just like that, all the months and years put in went out the window. No thank you, no goodbye, no anything. Effective immediately, just like that. The union rep and my ex-supervisor timidly said I had things at the school that I would need. The Personnel Director said okay, but I would have to be escorted back into the school after dismissal and supervised as I collected my things.

As I sat there, I was relieved and at peace all at the same time. Inwardly, I thanked God.

As I made my way home that afternoon and on opening my garage door, at around 12:30 p.m., I clearly said to God, *"If you allowed this to happen, I know it is for a higher purpose."* I called my then-husband, told him what had happened, and then called my Pastor. I went inside the house and went straight to bed. All was quiet on the news front for that evening.

A school that had been plagued with challenges for over a decade and a half, prior to me leading it, now had me as its fall girl.

Wednesday, April 6, 2016

By the end of the evening the following day, the local TV news reporters told the tale of how I had been suspended with pay as the supply teacher was accused of inappropriate behavior. The incident they said came on the heels of another where two students got into an altercation, and one student ended up being stabbed with a pen.

I stayed in bed all day on April 6, 2016, but on Thursday morning, April 7, 2016, I got up. I had work to do. In July 2009, I had been accepted into an Educational Leadership Doctoral Program. Students had a total of seven years to complete the degree. Here I was, almost seven full years in and had yet to defend my dissertation proposal, let alone finish and defend the dissertation.

God was on my side. He had a greater plan and a clear and definitive sense of humor. I would spend the next four and a half months of my paid administrative leave while they investigated me, going to the library five days a week to work on completing my dissertation.

I was reminded that ALL things work together for good to them that love God... and are called according to His purpose.

4

ANSWERING THE CALL: NAVIGATING ORDINATION

REV. JASSICA CASTILLO-BURLEY

"This is the church that you will be ministering in for the rest of your life."

It was a nice sunny day; my husband and I had just come home from church and were preparing Sunday lunch. My son was playing in the conservatory. I stopped what I was doing for a moment and had gone to the conservatory to check on him. Of course, he was fine. So, I returned to the kitchen and just as I entered through the door, I heard a voice: *"This is the church that you will be ministering in for the rest of your life"*. It was so loud that I said to my husband,

"Did you hear that?"

"Hear what?" he said.

"That voice", I replied.

"No, I didn't hear anything" was the answer.

Of course, he didn't hear it because it was God's direct

word for me, which I just couldn't believe. We spent the time preparing lunch, discussing these words and what exactly this all meant. My first impressions were that I heard this message for my husband. He had already secured a job in the Church of England, and it would be right for him to have a ministry there. He wasn't convinced that I had heard for him, and I was adamant that it couldn't possibly be for me.

Our journey so far had taken a turn. We had completed three years of Bible training and were wondering what would now happen. My husband had come to the end of his placement at the local Church of England, and we were seriously thinking about where God is going to bring us next. At morning prayer, I heard the church-warden praying for the new post they had just advertised for a family worker. As discreetly as I could, I nudged my husband and asked him what was that about? He had no idea, and in his own discreet way, was not ready to pursue it at this time. Prayer meeting or no prayer meeting, I needed to know.

So, long story short, he got the job, and the vicar was quite surprised as they had never employed anyone outside of the church who was not a member of the Church of England. One of the terms of his contract was that we were to be at all services and to be involved in the children's work. So, having to be at church every Sunday morning as a family was quite a stretch. Having both being brought up in a black Pentecostal church, entering this type of worship was quite different to what I was used to. Although they sang similar hymns, they sounded so different. It was mixed in with sung liturgy, which sounded so strange. There was no clapping or the odd person shouting out their praise to God. It was all very "proper".

However, being the woman that I am, I was going to take it as a time of learning and began reading books, going on courses, and asking all those awkward questions that people who were familiar with this life had taken for granted

I had always loved studying, and having completed my Bible training course, I was still ready to learn more. I studied for the Bishop's certificate and then went onto a pathways course. This was a course to find out what avenues of ministry that individuals could possibly be involved in. At this point, I wasn't interested in ministry but just an understanding of the liturgy, ways of worship, language, and rituals within this church.

On the pathways course, I learnt a lot about two subjects that were close to my heart: worship and prayer. For a whole year, I studied prayer, and for two years, I studied worship. After completing my studies, I was licensed as the first worship minister in the Diocese of Lichfield. At this point, I thought that was it. I had made it and could pursue leading worship, teaching worship, and all things worship with a foundation in prayer. What more could I have asked for?

I had arrived...

Or so I thought until...I heard the voice.

It didn't take us long to realise that the voice was meant for me. Following the afternoon service, I spoke to the vicar and explained to him what had happened earlier. To my surprise, he became quite animated and booked an appointment for me to see him the next day.

We had a nice chat, and then within a few days, I started my vocational journey within the Church of England.

Answering The Call

I was assigned to a vocational advisor, and we were set to meet once a month with tasks to complete between our meetings. I was so excited about the whole process that I did all that was required of me in good time. After a year and a half, I was transferred to another vocational advisor, who specialised in BAME (Black, Asian, & Minority Ethnic) candidates. Somehow, someone thought I needed to understand what it was like to be a black person in the Church of England and assigned me to visit a predominantly black church in (the Black country) West Bromwich, twice a month. I thought I had gone back in time. I would travel for nearly half an hour and be sitting outside the church building, waiting for folks to turn up. However, I was able, at least, to preach or teach or lead worship at each service. I was also able to help with their fundraising events. After some time, I began to get weary. This was heightened by the fact that someone persuaded my husband that he should also follow the ordination route, and he was fast-tracked through all the stages. At the last hurdle, he decided it wasn't for him and left with their blessing. (I knew it was for him all the time, but here I am...).

So, my vocational journey continued. After a year, I was getting a bit fed up, and my attitude began to get really bad. What was the point of all this? I would be retired before I actually got this post I really believed God had carved out for me. Did I really hear God, or was it just wishful thinking? Eventually, my attitude got the better of me, and soon, the vocational advisor suggested that I take some time off from pursuing my dream and 'find myself'.

My first thought was great, no more travelling up and down the M6 motorway, more time to spend with my family, and doing the things I really loved. At that point, it was the best thing she could have said.

However, the vicar was not happy. Spending time with him, I explained my frustrations to him, mentioning that although I was meant to minister in this church till the day I die, I didn't know how much longer I had to live (literally). A bit dramatic now, I look back, but at the time, it was just how I was feeling. I also felt that I was just wasting time. He spoke to the vocational advisors, explaining the above and once again, things started to move. Within a few months, I was back on track, awaiting my BAP (Bishop's Advisory Panel).

My BAP was on the 22nd of June 2015. This involved a weekend residential with one-to-one interviews, presentations, sermons, and pastoral exercises. Preparation beforehand included writing a personal written reflection based on mission and evangelism, filling in a CV, getting four references, obtaining a DBS check, fulfilling safeguarding criteria, and preparing a presentation with questions to spark a group discussion. Somehow, I had to prove that I was capable of carrying out the training required. I'm not sure how I did that, although to my credit, I do have a degree in Applied Chemistry. Every aspect of the weekend was scrutinised: breakfast, lunch, and dinner. You could just feel someone observing you. It's a good job. I was used to using a knife and fork and knowing about the order for using my cutlery.

Up until I arrived at the BAP, I was still unsure how this would work out. On my last meeting before the BAP, I was asked what my worst fear was. It was that I would feel so much out of my depth that I would clam up and not be able to speak or even be my true self. I was pleasantly surprised to find a card waiting for me with a word of encouragement to get me through. The scripture on the front said, *"You have not chosen me, but I have chosen you."* On the other side, it said, *"My prayer for you is that you will have such a sense of God's presence and peace that you will be able to be yourself, come away from this feeling you have said everything you needed to say, and then in the strength of His grace, leave the outcome to His wisdom."* Whenever I felt overwhelmed, I would return to my room, look at the card and go back to whatever was the next assignment.

Up until this point, I hadn't had the courage to tell anyone outside of my immediate family—not my mum, my sisters or any of my friends. What were they to think of this drastic move of mine? Did I really hear God? At this point, I was unable to vocalise what had happened on that Sunday afternoon many months before. However, if this BAP residential didn't work out, I would be free to carry on my life as if nothing had ever happened.

This was not to be. Less than a week later, I received the phone call from the bishop's office to say that I had passed all the criteria and that they were recommending me for ordination training. WHAT? HOW? WHY? NO WAY!!!

Looking back, I find that this situation I was going through must have been similar to Abraham when he had heard from God and had to tell his family that he was leaving.

"What d'you mean you're leaving?"

"Well, I heard from God and He asked me to leave!"

"Which God?"

"Leave and go where?"

"I'm not sure!"

"But we have always lived here, all of our ancestors are buried here!"

"I know...but something bigger than what I know is compelling me to do this!"

"I don't understand this!"

"Neither do I...but I'm sure it will make more sense as I begin to take my journey."

"Whatever you say..."

When my husband got home, I told him about the phone call from the bishop and he was really excited. Our son who would have been seven or eight was so excited that we were going on another adventure. Up until this point, he had lived in so many places. He was a true nomad.

My next challenge was telling my mum.

We arranged to visit her. On our arrival, we went through the usual formalities. Eventually, I just said, *"Mum, I am going for ordination in the Church of England."* I might as well have just announced a terminal illness.

After some time of silence, she said, *"What are the people going to say about this?"*

I couldn't believe that the first thing to come to her mind was what the folk at church would say about her daughter.

"But what do you think, mum? It doesn't really matter what others think..."

No reply. I never really knew what she thought until she turned up to my ordination service to deacon at Lichfield Cathedral. It all ended well.

Eventually, the rest of my family were told, and most of them were excited for me.

A New Direction

So, once again, we packed up our things and moved to Cambridge to attend Ridley Hall College. New school for my son, a new job for my husband, and studying for myself after not studying at university level education for over 20 years. I was trying to establish a new rhythm of life in a new place. Cycling... why didn't they mention we had to cycle from one building to the next? Another challenge to be conquered. I had not ridden a bicycle since I was 14, and back then, I didn't enjoy it. How was I going to enjoy this new challenge? I practised every evening after college until I felt confident, then took my bicycle to college and cycled with the rest of my class. They were a lot more confident than I was.

I spent two years of intense training at Ridley Hall, learning new patterns of worship, different theological understanding, making and building relationships, and having continuous fellowship with individuals that I possibly would never have met otherwise.

When I look back on my journey, I wonder if I had really thought about it whether I would have started. It reminds me of the scripture that says, *"And truly, if they had been mindful of that country from where they came out, they might have had opportunity to have returned"* (**Hebrews 11:15; KJV**).

I must admit that being ordained in the Church of England has been the best thing that I have ever done, apart from having my son. Why? Because I did it for me.

I challenged myself each step of the way—often feeling out of my depth; living with the not-knowing; concerns for my husband and son, and the helplessness of being an older person. I faced my own fears each step of the way. Fears of not being accepted; of being rejected by my roots, family, or church family; the strain on my son and husband; the fear of failure or not being enough. I triumphed over each obstacle every step of the way.

By learning to live in the now, to see God and allow Him to meet me in difficult situations, I learnt to be grateful and thankful in all circumstances—ultimately, the strength drawn from the voice I had heard right at the beginning. And now, I minister not only in the Church of England but in most denominations—leading worship, preaching, teaching, leading women's groups, running Bible studies, taking weddings, funerals, baptisms, christenings, and communion. Most importantly are the everyday pastoral meetings and bringing Jesus into the lives of all the people I meet.

I believe that I am paving the way for others to walk this road. To break down the walls and barriers that separate us as denominations and culturally, and to move out into what God is doing for this generation.

I return to my home church and the many churches where I once was a member, and they are so surprised to find out that the path that I have taken hasn't caused me to backslide, but it has propelled me into a new dimension of God's love and provision.

I am now faced with a new challenge. We are settled here, but we must move on. However, we have no way of knowing where to go. Job advertisements have been frozen or put on hold. So, I am left again with the feeling of not-knowing, not being needed or wanted, but I have heard the voice. So, this is what I hold onto.

However, I would like to give God thanks for this opportunity.

5

SILENCE IS NOT GOLDEN: NAVIGATING SHYNESS

RONA ANDERSON

"Train your mind to see the good in everything"- Anonymous

Being positive is a choice, and I choose to be happy. Our thoughts are wired into our mind and form pathways. The more you think about something, the more it will be imprinted in your mind!

There was a long period in my life when I thought, believed, and acted as though I was shy. Based on some of the accomplishments I am known for, it is hard to believe, but true. So, I will explain to you how I steered my life out of shyness.

- Me, the person who taught an aerobics class on the top of the Andes mountain range while trekking from Chile to Argentina.
- Me, the driver who when exhausted during a 100-mile journey in the early hours of the morning, encouraged my passengers to jump out

of the car at a service station car park and do high energy socarobics in the open to break up the monotony and stay awake.

- Me, the scholar who uninvited, boldly walked into a £1,000 per head conference in an exclusive London venue, and impressed the organisers so much that I was granted free entry.
- Me, the project manager who introduced herself to top psychologists, professors, therapists and trainers, then invited them to speak at a successful online well-being conference, empowering 500 families across the world.
- Me, the one who for the past 37 years has travelled worldwide and experienced many different cultures.

In toxic environments, I take delight in transforming the atmosphere with positive, encouraging words of affirmation whilst carrying a smile on my face. As a manager, I shielded my teams from negative aspects within organisations. I would read out positive encouraging quotes for the day. It could be bitter cold, windswept with my brolly blown inside out, pouring with rain, and I would be the one who walks in chirpily saying we need the rain. It is a beautiful day, and the wind allows the seeds to scatter, etc. I would pay complete strangers a compliment and derive pleasure seeing their initial shock turned into a smile.

Nevertheless, the label of shyness was deeply etched into my brain. If you, like me, are thinking the socially awkward label and the above accolades are not congruent, you are right. So, where did the shy association come from? How did I navigate my life to overcome it? I will now let you in on my secret.

Silence Isn't Golden; It's Awkward

For a period in my life, I was told to be silent, that I was a chatterbox and spoke jabberwocky. Whatever "jabberwocky" was, it did not appear to be a great language that one would be encouraged to learn. When you are told whenever you speak, it is nonsense, meaningless and incomprehensible, it feels hurtful and harmful. I was told I was annoying and too inquisitive, and hence, I clammed up.

It was the late 1970s, and I wasn't quite a teenager. I was embarking on puberty and was very impressionable. To curb my vocal irritations, I was told by those I respected and whose every syllable I clung, to speak only when spoken to. Like a sponge, I soaked this up, and the 'speak when spoken to' became transfixed in my mind. This became the most transformational message I had ever received at the time. It changed the course of my life and had a negative influence on the development of my character. Life and death are truly in the power of the tongue, and for a time, this maimed the real Rona.

Oh, I am sure there was rejoicing that the irritating little girl had now cemented this speak-when-spoke-to rule, and for a few days, there was some delightful peace as I took the rule into most situations. However, the shyness that also transpired was not bargained for.

As a young girl, the sceptical shopkeeper, Mr Fothergill, peered at me from behind the counter, infuriated, steam coming out of his ears, having had enough of me giving him the longest ever blank stare. You see, after being alerted to the speak-when-spoken-to rule, that could only be true if no one spoke. So, when I arrived at the corner shop, having taken the phrase literally, when Mr Fothergill said, *"Yes?"* I awaited and stared blankly. *Yes* could mean any manner of things. So, I continued to look straight at him.

This visit was like a comic scene from the Two Ronnies or Laurel and Hardy. Instead of walking into the shop and asking the shopkeeper for the tantalising sweets, I merely stood there. There was a long uncomfortable pause while he looked at me expectantly. Eventually, he said *"yes"* again. I still waited—another long pause. The puzzled shopkeeper asked me what was wrong with me. I answered him, *"Nothing"*; another long pause. I could see the frustration on his face. This communication or lack of went back and forth. *"Yes? What's wrong with you?"*, *"Nothing"*. He became so vexed he eventually slammed his fist on the counter and demanded, *"What can I get you?"*. At last, I was able to open up and speak, disclosing the long list of sweets! This became the manner of our regular miscommunication during each visit to the sweetshop.

Oh, She's The Shy One

This newfound attachment of shyness became like my new coat of armour, which I wore with pride. I thought it was great to be shy. People would say she's the shy one, and I would smile as though it was something to be proud of. However, it was an imposter, and I began to fear judgement from everyone.

Although, it was unlike the imposter of Impostor syndrome, where one compares and doubts the value of their skills and experience, fearing being exposed as a "fraud" though they are actually competent. The shyness I and others labelled me with was not actually me. The label was born out of fear, and it took me some decades to actually realise that the real imposter in the room was shyness. The imposter where I assumed a character and identity called shy, which was a deception of who I truly am.

This label manifested throughout the years in a variety of ways. Here are some of the many examples:

The imposter

After receiving my BA (Hons) degree, I won an award for Textile Designer of the year. Having never fainted in my life, due to the anxiety and fear brought on by this shy episode, my heart beat faster, blood drained from my face, and I fainted just as I was about to step on the podium at the Business Design Centre to collect my outstanding award.

Low Confidence

I was blessed with having wonderful males in my life whom I valued and respected. Therefore, manipulative relationship games were not my portion. I had a glowing relationship with my father, respected my brother, and bonded well with my nephews. I had platonic male friends, in whose company I felt comfortable, just so long as there was no romantic inkling whatsoever! However, if there were potential for them to be interested in me or vice versa, I would run a mile. I would admire people from a distance, and if they ever approached me with romantic intentions, ridiculous bumbling words would tumble uncontrollably from my mouth.

Procrastination; Lack of Self-esteem

Another low confidence episode arose when I attempted to finally meet my absolute all-time heartthrob; yes, Sir Tom Jones. I had the opportunity to meet him whilst in the audience of The Voice. By the time I plucked up the courage to stride over to him, I had stumbled and fell flat on my face, literally! Whilst in transit to the ground, I reached out, grabbing at something to keep me steady. Unfortunately, it was someone's long hair weave. Ouch, the pain!!! By the time I got back on my feet, my heart-throb has been whisked away, never to be seen again... Another missed opportunity.

Socially Awkward

One afternoon in my youth, I recall being invited to a family friend's house; my back remained glued to the living room wall. To this day, I have no explanation for doing that; the only reason could have been immense, extreme, and painful shyness.

I often hid behind the boisterous confidence of my friends who were always loud and outspoken. Although I had a loud voice, I was deemed quiet. I developed pride in being shy and labelled as such. For the bulk of my life, I wore the shy badge. I polished it. It gleamed brightly. It shone. No one wore that badge with greater pride than me. I was painstakingly shy.

But that shyness was just a badge. With my inner circle of people who invested in seeing the real Rona, I removed the badge, putting it back on afterwards. I was shy, but I'm the first and last person on the dance-floor. Oh, I hate public speaking, but I wouldn't hesitate when asked to deliver a sermon to hundreds of people and do an altar call during my first mission trip to Africa. I have since gone on to be an intrepid missionary on ten trips to various parts of Africa to be of service to the poor.

I never avoided social situations. In fact, I was a very sociable person. Although when I went out, I hid behind others, allowing my friends to take centre stage. I felt safe when I was out with my male friends, as a masculine vibe was sent out, which warned the opposite sex off, forming a protective barrier. I was relieved there was a reluctance to approach me as I had that invisible sign of "look but do not dare touch". I was shy out of fear, concerned about what other people may think of me or getting things wrong, and therefore, being rejected. I was overprotective of myself. There was even a stage when I put weight on, hoping that I could hide behind the extra pounds.

I could effortlessly strike up a conversation with a complete stranger on a train. I could do that because I thought I would never see that person again.

Unfortunately, shyness soon closed many open doors. It closed potential relationships. It closed opportunities for excellent career roles. Then, a conversation with a great orator who I value and respect, completely transformed my outlook and the trajectory of my life. The penny dropped. Shackles were removed. Scales were shed, and the authentic Rona was released when I realised I no longer had to wear the imposter's coat.

When I took a personality test, to my horror, the strange thing is that it stated I was more extroverted than introverted. I found that hard to believe. How could someone labelled as shy be an extrovert? I then realised that shyness is not related to being an introvert. Introverts get their energy by being alone or in quiet places. This was not the case with me as I actually wanted to connect with other people, but I really did not know how as I was so used to taking the easy route of staying in the background. Shy people fear being judged negatively. Notice the difference.

"Shyness is when you turn your head away from something you want" - Jonathan Safran Foer, Novelist.

How many times had I turned away or turned my back on something I wanted!? That conversation, that lead, that development, that friend, that promotion—countless.

The Breakthrough

The great orator, Bishop Wayne Malcolm, gave me a springboard to a breakthrough by alerting me that shyness is fear.

*"For God did not give us a spirit of fear, but **of power and love and of a sound mind"** -2* Tim. I v. 7 (NKJV)

If God did not give it to me, I did not want it. This was a positive transformational message, hitting me like a bolt of lightning. Shyness is a negative attribute, not the positive one I thought was great to hide behind. I took control and chose not to be shy. Life and death are in the power of the tongue, and you shall be whatever you call yourself to be. So, I now refuse that label. I don't want it, and I will not claim it. It is not my portion. I have a choice to label myself in the way God labels me, and when I meet people who make the same mistake as me and try and label themselves inappropriately, I encourage them otherwise.

A label is an attachment that indicates the manufacturer, size, destination, and care of a product. Did the shy label indicate my manufacturer, creator God? My size or stature? Where I'm going in life? How to care for myself? No way!!! So, what did I have to believe to remove the negative label and put on the positive? We need to ask that question of our beliefs. Many of our limiting beliefs are not true. As such, draw a line under them, move on, and write a new one.

You can't undo what has gone before, but you can create new experiences, memories, and pathways in your brain. That's what I had to do. Therefore, I trained my mind to purposefully build the habit of looking for positives. I classify that period of the shy label as protection, and I have drawn a line under it, writing a new label of authenticity.

A New Label

I call myself what I want to be and define myself as who I am. Uniquely me.

I stopped allowing the inner critic to whisper negative things in my ear about who I am.

I know who God says I am.

I have fun in all I do.

I don't give credit to shyness. If I mess up, I mess up. I don't fall back on shyness or use it as a crutch or excuse for bad behaviour.

I am unfazed by other people's opinions of me and realise that people like me for being me, and if they do not, if they have a negative view of me, then that's their issue, not mine.

I made a commitment to myself to turn up as Rona Anderson every day.

Authenticity Unveiled

I embraced my vulnerability, and I'm willing to let others see the real authentic Rona. I became proud of who I actually am.

"If someone offers you an amazing opportunity and you are not sure if you can do it, say yes—then learn how to do it later!" - Sir Richard Branson.

I adopted this approach in life. I refuse to say I will not do something because of shyness. When I am asked to do things that I have never done before, I say, *"Yes, sure I can do it"*. Like writing in this anthology, I said *"yes"*. So, there is no room for shyness to reappear and attempt to take hold of me as an imposter in my life. I don't have time to be shy or wallow in self-pity. Do you realise shyness takes up so much energy which you could use on something else? Just do it and forget to be shy.

I stopped thinking of what could go wrong if I stepped out and started thinking of the wonderful opportunities and open doors if things went right. I have nothing to lose.

The label of shyness was focused on me, but I shifted the focus away from me. I became happy to be vulnerable. I am willing to let others see the real me. Being genuine and vulnerable is often the quality that others appreciate about me. I now 'DO IT'.

Do

Own

Incredible

Thoughts

The shy badge has been shredded. I arrive early at venues in order to settle and dismiss any social anxiety, with some small talk ready and prepped in my mind. I believe in myself and now open up, and even if what I have to say is not in keeping, I still say it. There is no wrong question. Shyness is not my identity. Now, I am the authentic me—positive with bags of energy.

Sometimes, I do slump back into that comfortable, secure cotton wool fortress of a risk-less person. But I know it is an imposter. When the shy Rona rears its ugly head, I identify it and call it what it is, an imposter and try to live less in that space. In fact, I do not own that label. I no longer call myself shy, and I refuse to allow others to give me that label. The Rona I love is free, bold, and courageous.

The real Rona Anderson has unveiled herself—Happiness Consultant helping people improve their happiness; an International Development Partnerships Manager speaking at over 30 annual events releasing children from poverty; a Project Manager providing well-being initiatives to support the local community, and Director of Global Missions developing hearts for overseas missions. They all have one thing in common—Improved Well-being. God created me to improve the well-being of those in need, which is what I dedicate my life to, leaving the label of shyness firmly behind me.

Apparently, four out of ten people consider themselves shy. I am delighted to be in the 60% who do not.

Take Control And Choose To Be Happy

Speak when spoken to meant that someone had to break the silence, and I handed that responsibility to others instead of taking control of my own joy. It prevented me from showing up as my real self. I want to empower you to recognise your own responsibilities, nurture the new, and authorise your own happiness. I have focused on dismantling one label. But there are many labels that enhance limiting beliefs, and my passion is to remove every limiting belief.

Give yourself positive labels; see the good in you and choose to be happy.

6

SURVIVING SEXUAL ASSAULT: NAVIGATING HEARTBREAK TO GOD'S LOVE

NADINE FORDE

My 40th birthday was approaching, and I wanted to do something special to celebrate this landmark. My thirties were drawing to a close, and I was genuinely relieved about it—no more mistakes. Forties, here I come. Life, as they say, begins at forty after all! This new chapter would be a fresh start and a new beginning. I debated two options, a lavish party or a relaxing Caribbean holiday. The latter seemed obvious; my lifelong best friend, Pamela, now resided in the Caribbean, and a few distant family members. It would cater to my needs, sun, and a good time around loved ones. My latest relationship had hit the rocks, and I was jaded by the cycle of breakup and reconciliation. What better excuse to brush away the remnants of disappointment?

The sweltering sun engulfed me as I stepped off the aeroplane. I took a deep breath and hoped the next four weeks would be a time of pampering and putting myself first for a change. In hindsight, I was an unloved, insecure woman who just yearned for real, true deep love. Really and truthfully, my life seemed to have come to a halt at thirty, when my beloved mother passed suddenly. She was my best friend, my confidante, my everything; so you could say, I was turning thirty again.

I spent my birthday on the beach, with a good book and a large floppy hat, soaking up the sun and listening to the waves lap softly on the sand. It was paradise. I could stay here forever. It had been so long; I just loved being in Pamela's company again. Her beautiful daughter, Emily, who I had not seen since birth, was now a walking, talking, inquisitive toddler who loved to make us laugh and toddle around in my highest heels...quite well, I might add. Pamela and I loved catching up on life; we just enjoyed being two peas in a pod. She had moved to the Caribbean a year earlier for a fresh new start and had acquainted herself with the island again. Before her emigration, she frequented the island every year. At her lovely mountaintop apartment, the evenings were filled with the colourful rhythms of steel pans. I noticed a real change in her since she moved. We were both healing from breakups and seeking meaning in life once again.

She had a friend named Webster, who was a visually impaired male massage therapist. He was part of our Tour Guide and a new friend. Webster was charming. I admired how his disability didn't hinder his goals and how he willed it into a positive, successful career path. I got to know him and trusted him like a big brother. So, when he introduced me to his friend and driver—Roman —a good looking, dark, smooth-skinned, softly spoken man; I had no reason to doubt Webster. I plunged head-first and head over heels into a holiday romance. I became the lead in my own romantic movie.

We quickly became inseparable, and he would drive us everywhere. Our dates were incredible. One night in particular, we ate a beautiful lobster dish renowned on the island, followed by cocktails at a beautiful seafront restaurant and bar. We lounged on the balcony whilst the waves crashed below us. The sound of the sea and light breeze alone lulled me into a sense of security. This was just what I thought I needed. We ended the evening with a stroll along a nearby private beach solely used for the preservation of giant sea turtles. We waited to see the hatched baby turtles make their way out to sea. It was captivating and the most enchanting way to end a wonderful evening. Maybe...he could be the one. Because of past relationships, I was still wary and a little guarded. But how could I resist the pull of being in love and possibly finally finding my soul mate in the Caribbean? Were my bad relationships a thing of the past? I was desperate for love and security. Only two weeks into the holiday, I should not have ignored the speed with which this relationship gained momentum. You know what they say about driving too fast? You might crash.

A few days before my departure from the island, Roman surprised me. He asked me to be his wife! I was stunned yet on cloud nine. This was it—no time to think logistics just yet, wedding plans, visas, time frame, or mindset. I was getting married! We would plan over the next few months, and I didn't mind funding the majority financially. I had a decent well-paid job as a Consultant contractor.

On reflection, it wasn't a real proposal, more of a statement. Maybe, I was just in love at the thought of finally being married and having a husband. Anyway, all his friends congratulated him, Webster being one of the first, compared to some of my close friends who had genuine reservations. *"Too much, too soon, too fast,"* they shouted! I ignored them all.

1 Peter 5:8 (NIV): *Be alert and of sober mind. Your enemy the devil prowls around like a roaring lion looking for someone to devour.*

I returned to London in a whirlwind. There was so much to arrange. Roman didn't want to wait and would arrive in a couple of months. I wrote his letter of invitation so he could get his visitor's visa, initially, three to six months. It was sorted, as I utterly ignored the red flags that were being waved frantically before my very eyes. My inside voice screamed, *"Break this off, woman; it's gone too far. You can turn back, you know!"* But instead, I chose to override the voice of what seemed like doom and proceeded to try on wedding dresses, choose bridesmaids, seek flower arrangements and venues. Before sending financial help for part of Roman's fare, I must admit I had cold feet.

The day came when I would collect Roman from the airport. I was excited, but a distant sobering thought crossed my mind. *"What if I have made a really huge mistake?"* Just then, I looked up, and a beaming smile hit me like a ton of bricks. I felt immeasurable guilt. *"Let me make this work"*, I reasoned. I was in a good job and could hold things down whilst he was here. We hugged and made our way home. During our conversations, I noticed there was no sense of urgency for him to make plans for our future. No talk of marriage, no ambition, nothing. Was I overthinking this? Unsure and full of guilt, he persuaded me to be intimate with him that night, even though I had my doubts in the back of my mind. I suddenly started to feel uncomfortable, but I thought it was me being overly cautious. *"Relax,"* I thought to myself. I just had to relax. Everything would be all right.

The next day, distracted, I was livid as I saw a live cockroach in the kitchen, obviously from his luggage and packaging. I quickly got rid of the offending creature, cleaned and disinfected the house. Thankfully, it worked, but it left me irritated. I scolded myself. *"I should have more patience"*, I whispered. A few days had passed, and we seemed to settle into some semblance of a routine when I broached questions about our future. He told me, *"Well, you are my wife already, so we don't need to get married!"* *"Huh?"* I cried, *"What do you mean?"* My fairytale started to unravel before my very eyes.

There was a local pub at the end of my road, and he seemed to spend all day there, drinking ale and watching sports. All those behaviours were new to me. Who was this Roman? He was alien to the man I had met on the island. After a full day's work, he expected me to cook, clean, and cater to his every whim. Umm no...this isn't what I expected or could tolerate. I decided to have a lengthy chat with him but to no avail. Roman had not a care in the world about what I had to say; it was all about him. I realised then it is better to get out of this as quickly as I leapt in.

Work was exhausting, and after a hard day, I just wanted to sleep, but I was determined to end things. Roman had to leave. He had to go. That way, I thought he could still enjoy his time here and return to the island early. I had made a hash of this so-called relationship. It was a phenomenal mistake. I knew it was time to sort this out in the most considerate and final way possible. He needed to hear me this time, that it was a mistake. We needed to break things off and that I would drive him to stay with his friends across the other side of London. He begged me to stay, but I stood firm and made him a bed on the sofa. I knew our paths in life were different, but he could stay until the end of the week. My decision was final; I felt a huge sigh of relief. I got ready for bed, as I had work in the morning.

Being so incredibly tired, my body started to drift off, but I heard faint creeping footsteps ascending the stairs through my groggy state. The house was in total darkness. Roman entered my room and immediately began pleading for forgiveness. In my exhaustion, I thought he would know it is fruitless trying to convince me otherwise. If only he could just leave me alone. He said, *"I know what you need"*. He roughly pulled back my covers and proceeded to climb into my bed. I don't want to argue, and I definitely don't want any form of intimacy. My mind was racing; *is this how he wanted to resolve the matter?* Suddenly, he pinned my arms down on the bed. I gasped. This could not be happening to me, in my house, in my room, in my bed? Using all my strength, I couldn't fight him off. I panicked; he was stronger than I anticipated, and I struggled. *"What do you think you're doing?"* I shouted. I tried to scream, but the noise wouldn't come out. I mistakenly thought I could end this, but he was far too strong. I went into shock and just lay there, limped, as he raped me in silence. I was numb. *Was this real life? Was Roman raping me?* He was a monster; I really didn't know him at all. A stranger was violating me. I pleaded for the ordeal to be over. He thought he did nothing wrong and went back downstairs quietly to sleep. I couldn't sleep that night; I was scared, confused, shocked, petrified, angry, and shaking. I felt ashamed.

Sleep evaded me; my alarm startled me. Still in shock and trembling, I slowly descended the stairs. He was asleep. Void of emotion, I got ready for work. He had to leave today! How I managed to work through that day still astounds me, but I left early, feeling nauseous, vomiting, and retching on the way home. I was a mess. I couldn't go home. I was a nervous wreck; he had a spare key! In sheer panic, I rang one of my best friends, Rebekah. Her voice was the voice of calm and reason, *"Babes, oh my God, this is horrific. Try and calm down; I'm so sorry you had to endure this. You have to ring the police now and have him arrested!"* Her directness woke me out of my slumber. Shaking, I called the police and told them about the incident. They would have a squad car with two officers at my home in 30 mins, they assured me. It was the longest, most overwhelming, and painful drive home of my life. The officers were waiting as I parked. It was a relief to have them inside the house with me. They took my statement and confirmed he would be arrested and taken into custody upon arrival. My nerves failed me, and I was extremely jumpy even with the two officers present. A pizza pamphlet fluttered through the letterbox and floated onto my floor. I froze. The female officer touched my shoulder to reassure me. Five minutes passed, then ten, then fifteen. A key turned in the door, and in he walked, as if nothing had happened. The policewoman asked, *"Are you Roman Browne?"* *"Yes, that's me,"* he looked bewildered. The police were swift and arrested him on the spot, handcuffed him, and read him his rights. They handed me back my spare keys. The relief and yet unexplained shame I felt, at that moment, as they led him to the squad car in handcuffs. He was gone, for now. After they left, I collapsed onto the sofa, sobbing uncontrollably. Another close friend, Francine, rushed over to console me and help me pack all his belongings to deposit at the police station. I exhaled. He was in custody, but a looming dark cloud had entered my life that would consume me.

The police called me in for an interview to inform me of my options and told me he would be released on bail. They couldn't keep him in custody. They advised me that if I wanted to go ahead, he would have to stay in the country for six months to a year to see if the case would be taken up by the Crown Prosecution Service. Another option is that he could leave the country voluntarily within a week. I was too afraid. It was like this chapter in my life had been engraved on my mind. Fearful, I dropped the charges. I wanted to go ahead with the case but couldn't cope with him being in the country. He left England. The officers said I would have had a hard time in the courts too. My world crumbled; I was inconsolable. Hastily, I changed my number as I started to receive anonymous threatening calls. I just wanted the trauma to end. I proceeded to tell my family, and I felt as though they dismissed it, not acknowledging the devastating truth. Crushed again, I felt so upset, disappointed, and let down. My voice was silenced; no one could hear my heart's cry and screams.

There is a Saviour – *Come to me, all you who are weary and burdened, and I will give you rest.* Matthew 11:28 (NIV).

I was broken inside, so when a past love, Clive, came back into my life, I pretended to be fine. Clive knew what happened, but he never believed me. Part of me died inside, and I just detached myself from any form of emotion. I couldn't erase this episode of my life. My mind got blacker and deeper into a depression. Another layer of trauma curled around me. How would I navigate my way through the constant gnawing at my insides? Suicidal thoughts tormented me daily; I meticulously and methodically tried to plan it and would go over differing scenarios. It became an obsession. Would I swallow pills and wait for my life to ebb away or slash my wrists in the bath? Often, I would find myself speeding in my car alone and imagine driving into a wall. I had no support with how to deal with the unending pain, and truthfully, I didn't know how and where to seek help. The dark abyss was beckoning me, allowing me to feel that this was the only way. *"Come on, climb in; everything is going to feel better,"* it coaxed.

Light in my life came in the form of my lifelong supportive friends, Rebekah and Daniel. Both were beautiful people. They both knew Jesus Christ and encouraged me to get to know Him, go to church, find Him in Salvation.

I felt stronger, resisted the pull of darkness, and decided to worship with Rebekah at her church. This was my last hope. You see, I believed in God, but I started to doubt there was a God when the incident happened. How could it happen to me? Didn't God love me? Was there a God? As soon as I settled into Pastor George's sermon for the first time, God's Word jumped out at me and made me feel as if I was floating. The scriptures came alive; God's voice was clear. Yes…God is real; He was the lover of my soul. God loved me unconditionally, and He wanted a personal relationship with me. Something was breaking and clearing on the inside of me.

During the sinner's prayer of Salvation, my only and perfect option was to accept the call to receive Jesus Christ as my Lord and Saviour. He died at the cross, so I could live an abundant life, an eternal life, not just to exist. That day changed my very existence; the dark cloud and the engulfing abyss dissipated, and the Lord stepped in and comforted me with His everlasting arms. A broken and contrite heart He will not despise. I was somebody; I had a purpose, a hope, and a future. I had a voice; I was set free. No more depression; suicidal thoughts ceased. A huge wave of peace and joy washed over my body. He was my path to healing and could deliver me from all evil. I entered under the wings and shadow of the Almighty and had yet to discover the life God had for me. I took up my cross and followed Jesus. What did God have in store for me to do on this journey?

2 Corinthians 5:17 (NIV): *Therefore, if anyone is in Christ, the new creation has come: The old has gone, the new is here.*

7

NO TEARS: NAVIGATING MY DREAM
JULIE BRAHAM

England, West midlands in the late 60's: A group of men have gathered on the corner of the street, as a man walked past the group of men they began chanting *'Go HOME'* the man ran as fast as he could. Seeing his house at the end of the street he knew he could make it. He breathed a sigh of relief, my father was home, then there was an earth shattering noise of glass and screams. Then, discovering a brick had been flown through the window narrowly missing my sister in her cot.

My parents left their home in Jamaica to make a better life in the UK; both very hard-working. My mother gave up her place to be a midwife because she was pregnant with me, so when I heard that story I knew she did not give up her dream in vain.

My earliest memory was one cold October, standing in the front room watching the flames of the coal fire burn. My mother walked in and softly called my name, "Veron and Sharon gone". Still looking in the flames of the open fire, I looked down at my navy box pleated school skirt, I was silent *NO TEARS*. Later on in life, my mum wondered why I didn't cry at losing my two sisters on the same day, just one hour apart from each other.

As a child, we never lacked anything. In the summer holidays my father would drive to a seaside location with our cousins. Friday nights, dad would bring fish, chips and crisps. We had to scramble for our favourite flavour; mine was cheese and onion, but ended up with salt and vinegar. I can honestly say we never went without. We always had Christmas and birthday presents. I remember the brush nylon nighties and the half-slips made by my mom. *Happy no tears.*

School

Secondary school was fun. I was one the first pupils to attend a school which was previously a grammar and high school. It was in the local newspaper for the wrong reason due to the new diverse mix the pupils. I represented my school in the athletics team for 400-metres hurdles and I was on the netball team. *Happy no tears.*

On career day, I remember going to the office, excitedly telling the teacher of my dream of becoming a nurse. She looked up over her half-rimmed glasses, dressed in her twinset camel cardigan and tweed skirt with a smirk on her face and said *"You can't become a nurse; you will end up working in a factory."* I left her office broken and crushed; her words hit me like a slap. I ran home, hoping she didn't ring my mother and tell her. I opened the back door, which was always open unless both my parent were at work. My mother was in the kitchen; I could smell the patties she'd just taken out of the oven. When I told her what the teacher had said, she looked at me and said in her soft Jamaican accent, *"Never mind. If you put your mind to it, you can be anything you what to be."* Those words have always stuck with me, she believed in me.

When I left school, they recommended someone with my abilities should attend a youth opportunity scheme for six months. I left school with good grades in sociology and English literature; the rest were average. My first pay was £50, which I gave to my mother. She smiled and told me to keep it for myself. I wanted to help as my father worked long hours and come home with £50 pounds a week to feed our growing family.

Living The Dream

I went through my teen years being over looked and feeling like I wasn't good enough. That conversation on careers day was playing at the back of my mind, but my mother's words were louder. I decided not to apply for nursing school instead I went college full time for one extra year to gain extra qualifications.

Finally, the day came when I applied to nursing school, and I got accepted. When the letter came, I waited for my mother to come home and showed her the letter. I remember the smile on her face. Now I would start living my dream and fulfilling my mother's lost dream.

Blast From The Past

So the day came. I was on my last placement in A/E when

a woman was wheeling in, and I was assigned to do her observations. I drew back the curtains and introduced myself (even though we wore names badges). The women looked up and me with a look of shock and confusion on her face, her mouth open wide. She said my name twice as the penny dropped.

Right then my mind flashed back to careers day, where I heard the words, *"You will never be a nurse you will end up in a factory"*. And there she was, and here I was, standing there, I had a dream and I fulfilled it, despite her words.

I made sure I did everything I was taught, not forgetting to ask permission if I could do her observations, I don't want any complaints (but to be honest, I have never had any complaints from any patients for the whole of my nursing journey). And this teacher thought I couldn't do this! I made sure I did it right, I did it slower and smiled more, throughout it all she remained silent with her eyes upwards.

As I left her cubicle, my heart was beating fast. I felt like running, but I didn't...

No tears. I paused, looked up and said quietly, "Thank you."

Nursing

My first nursing role after qualifying was on a medical ward. I loved it. One afternoon, I was asked to do the ward rounds by the ward sister. I made sure I understood all the handover notes for each patient. As we introduced the next patient, when discharge was mentioned I would ask about housing and family support, this was met with blank stares from the consultant to junior doctors, so I stopped.

We got to another patient and the consultant asked me *"Nurse, what are her home circumstances like?"* with some hesitation I answered. As the consultant rushed out he paused and said *"Well done nurse"* I said thank you but his bleep was going off in his white coat so he didn't hear the answer. I thought someone is actually listening, I am being heard. 18 months later my opinion counts. Once again I paused, looked up and said *"Thank you."*

London

I took a bold step left my contracted job to move to South London for an agency position. I got offered a place and then heard all the nursing accommodation was named after English Poets. I knew this was the right move because I love poems. The hospital was nothing like the previous one. Here, I saw people like me, I got excited!

Within six months I was offered a permanent position and got a place on a conversion course, (I didn't think I was good enough for level 1, so opted for level 2). My ward manger questioned why I wanted to change, as she thought I was happy and well suited to that role. But, I don't want to be overlooked, passed by or unheard.

It took another 12 months for me to gain that level 1 nursing (registered nurse conversion) but it was so worth it.

On my first morning working in theatres as part of my rotation, I got to work 30 minutes early and walked up to two staff members. One of the women saw me approaching and said "*Oh, you want these,*" and she took out a hefty bunch of keys and placed them in my hand. I felt elated and had a spring in my step. I was in charge, and I had to open up the department.

I quietly introduced myself to the staff member when she looked at me and said, "*Oh, I thought you were...*" and then she looked at the two women who looked like me in the corridors, emptying the bins.

I was immediately transported back to the office at school; the feelings of not being good enough washed over me. Here I was, still having to prove myself.

It turned out this particular staff member was the theatre manager, and she treated all staff who looked like me in this demeaning manner. I decided not to complete my full rotation there, as nothing I did was good enough. The theatre manager gave me all the horrible jobs to do, but I did them and said nothing because I knew this would not be forever. I wondered if she was related to that teacher... *No tears, just frustration.*

Unexpected early delivery

Friday 13th is a day I will never forget. Just one month after completing my nursing, in this very hospital that I now work in. I had this excoriating pain in my stomach, being 6 months pregnant I knew that was not normal. I was giving birth prematurely. As I lay there in the maternity room, the doctors tried to delay labour but this child was determined to be birthed today!

Afterwards, I sat there, staring at my daughter, born three months early. I looked at this tiny girl in the Special Care Baby Unit, skin translucent, wearing a pink bonnet. I watched her chest slowly breathing. Suddenly, interrupted by a vicar, a tall man with thick brown hair carrying a bible - and something else in his hand that I couldn't quite make out. He smiled and asked, *"Do you want me to baptise your baby?"*

"No" I said. He had been sent by the staff as I was told she only had 72 hours to live - having given birth at six and a half months.

I held her hand. TEARS ran down my cheeks. She is going to live, I believed, and she is going to part of my journey in life!

My daughter left the Special Care Baby Unit Healthy!

Saying "No" to the vicar that day meant I had hope for her future and I knew she would be healthy. I had faith enough to know God would not take my child away in 72 hours like the medical staff had predicted.

I gave birth to my daughter in the same hospital I was working in, which was the same hospital I had just completed my registered nurse conversion course. I was filled with an incredible sense of achievement, emotions and love. Looking back, I now think all that had happened, was meant to be.

A New Season

I decided to changed direction in my nursing career. I left working in the hospital and went to work in a rehabilitation centre. It was the best move. The role gave me so much more opportunities and within six months I was qualified. I taught gentle exercises to older, less able people.

I was also given the opportunity to become a N.V.Q (national vocational qualification) clinical assessor. Working with my first student was such a joy and she then passed her N.V.Q.

Then a community hospital, with an attached rehabilitation centre was looking for assistant managers. The teams of nurses were all asked if they were interested and I thought, *this is mine, I'm taking it.* This position was just what I needed to propel myself forward and the bonus was that I would get to teach students on the ward. Sharing my skills and bringing the best out of people is such a joy to me.

My nephew was admitted to this hospital and I was called on many times for his care. I believe God had opened that door of opportunity and it worked in my favour!

What I have learnt

My mother would read Psalm 121 every night before she went to bed. *I lift up mine eyes unto the hills, from whence cometh my help...* Back then I didn't understand why but now I do. Her faith kept her going, just like my faith has kept me going and still is.

I am still in a job that I love and in a position to pass on my nursing skills.

I have found my voice. Now if I'm overlooked I change position or leave the environment to somewhere I will be noticed. I am now an active member of the Royal College of Nursing.

People say I'm quiet but I'm a thinker, I have grown and I am no longer running. My journey is not over.

You have to BELIEVE in yourself! There were parts of my life that were unbearable, like caring for both my parents till the end, then, I lost them both.

From my mother I learnt to never give up on my dreams and from my father I learnt to be resilient and to stay emotionally strong, even if doors are not opened, keep on knocking.

I have learned to be amongst like-minded people. Even when I found myself in meetings were everyone was a manager, a head of department or way above my grade, it didn't matter, because one day, I knew I would become a leader too.

8

IT IS ALL IN THE MIND: NAVIGATING MINDSETS

LARA SAMUEL

There is the saying, *'It is all in the mind',* but now I know my mind plays tricks on me.

I remember myself just two years ago, with insecurities, self-esteem issues and the feeling that I did not have a voice.

Today, as I reflect on my journey, I see how my mind has changed and evolved. I now stand tall as I look into the future. I feel confident and expectant of what the future holds. A few years ago, all this was locked away inside me, but now, I can shout it out, that it feels good to be 'Out' and 'Free'.

Okay, let us start from the beginning of my journey.

I moved to England with my husband, Michael, about 13 years ago. I can still remember it like yesterday. The decision to emigrate was an easy one because Michael and I wanted a new life and the best opportunity for our children.

Even though the decision was right for us, it was not easy to leave the place I had called home for over twenty years of my life.

I grew up in a large family, and they were happy with our decision to emigrate to the UK. However, they were concerned with how we would settle into a new life in the UK, but like most well-meaning families, they agreed with our decision.

I was concerned too, but I had to keep a bold and happy face and stand by our decision. I held that bold face until I got on the plane, but once we sat down, I cried all the way from Nigeria to England.

Life In England

I was happy with the decision to leave Nigeria, yet I cried. I cried for the life I was leaving behind, and I cried for the unknown life I was starting in the UK. It was the life I chose, yet I cried. I felt like I was crying because I knew I would lose a part of myself, although I did not know how much of myself I would lose.

Looking back now, I can see that coming to England was like having a clean slate.

I had so much to learn about the British way of life; my mind needed moulding.

Unfortunately, the kind of moulding, advice, and imprint I had was from family and friends who had their own mindset about the UK. It was based on other people's 'generational trauma and bias', and had I let those words shape my mindset. Advice such as:

'You just have to survive'.

'Keep your head down'.

'You are not going to work to make friends.'

'If you don't get an opportunity, it is because you are BLACK.'

'Don't bother to try to move up. Just do more shifts to make more money.'

'Work very "HARD" (in fact, ten times harder than white colleagues).'

All these became my formula for success in England.

Settling in England was not easy, and it was not cheap. It was lonely, even though I had my husband with me. It was difficult to step out the door of our home sometimes, with the look of 'YOU are different' on people's faces. It was difficult to speak sometimes because when I did, people would tell me, 'I don't understand what you are saying'. This used to make me so angry, and so I decided to 'speak less'.

A year after we arrived in the UK, our first daughter Hannah was born. I became preoccupied in the home taking care of her. I didn't have to go out much except to go to church or shopping.

Our family continued to grow as we welcomed our daughter, Elizabeth, and our son, Jeremiah. As our family grew, I knew I could not hide away in the house forever. I had to venture into the outside world, and I did.

Stepping out to go to work brought back the advice I had been given about survival in the UK.

When I started work, I worked in the NHS. Every day, I stepped out to go to work like I was going to 'war'. This war was a story I had developed in my mind. I had a routine to prepare myself for war. Every day, I would pack my hair up; that was a big thing for me. I just could not go to war (work) with my hair down; that was my mask.

At work, I would fake 'stupidity'. I had a first degree in Sociology, so of course, I am not stupid. However, based on situations at work, I sometimes felt that I needed to act like I didn't know things. I felt I couldn't show that I had different ideas or better ideas, especially if they were different from that of the manager. I would tell myself, *'They don't want to hear what I know or have to say'.*

It was easy for people to maltreat me because I would not object or complain. And when I shared ideas on a one-to-one basis, and someone took the idea as theirs, I would not oppose it. All I was there for was to do my work and leave. No time for chit-chat (Remember the advice, *'You are not going to work to make friends'*?). Secretly, I watched people who talked in the corridor about their weekend or evening plans, but I just assumed they were not serious workers.

Time For A Change

In 2019, something changed for me. I was still working in the NHS, but I had started taking training opportunities. Some of the training I had to pay for myself, but I started believing in myself again. By July of 2019, I got another job within the NHS, which was a promotion, and this ended up being a fantastic opportunity for me.

The new team, new manager, and new training programs made me question the mindset I had held on to since arriving in the UK. With this new team, I started speaking up more, and I was not faking stupidity as I did before. I still wore my hair tied up every day in preparation for war; I just couldn't let my hair down. The mask, to some extent, was still on.

As I started the year 2020, I know things were changing in the way I was 'thinking', but I didn't know how much more things would change for me. I was open to the idea of improving and re-educating myself. I attended training at work that was specifically for ethnic minority groups. The training blew my mind and crushed every single formula I had for success in the UK. It truly showed me that there is a lot of work to be done to improve race relations and racism in the UK but also pinpointed work for me to do.

After this training, I went back to work with a changed mindset. The hair was still tied up, but I was gradually becoming more confident in who I was. As I did for the first few times, I let my hair down to go to work. It felt so weird. It felt like I was naked without my mask. Even my daughter, Hannah, noticed I was letting my hair down, and she asked me if I was going to church. It showed me that my children had noticed the difference in me.

The more I let my hair down, the more I felt free at work —free without the mask; free to be me. I saw a difference in my demeanour; my family saw a difference, and even my colleagues at work noticed a difference in me.

Then the pandemic hit, lockdown and working from home started. Fortunately for me, I had worked hard at changing my mindset, which positively affected my mental health. By the time I started working from home, I had started genuinely enjoying my job. Of course, there were days when I felt down, but I knew the techniques to pick myself up again. For those days, I had systems around me to help pick me up. Some of those were my family, church family, and sisterhood from the Navigating Life Group.

I now have a whole new mindset. Whether I'm in or out of the office,

- I no longer see going to work like going to war.
- I no longer have to pack my hair up or wear a mask to go to work.
- I no longer just survive at work; I thrive.
- I no longer keep my head down; I explore possibilities.
- I now have friends at work.

- If I don't get an opportunity, I don't conclude that it's because I am Black. I go back, reflect, and learn from it; then I TRY AGAIN.
- I work SMART.

With my new mindset, I feel healthier and happier.

I think if people who knew me from Nigeria saw me now, they would recognise me, but if people in the UK had known me a few years ago, they probably would not recognise me.

Fast forward to March 2021; I now run a registered charity in the UK. I have set up a coaching business, I have had promotions at work, I am a speaker, and now soon-to-be author. It is an amazing feeling to be Out and Free.

Can you imagine the emotional fatigue and exhaustion I was exerting every day by going to work with this mindset? I was psychologically exhausted; even the act of preparing for the 'daily war' was draining. The act of wearing the mask to go to work and taking it off when I got home was wearing me down.

If I have learnt anything on my journey of re-educating my mind, it is that it is a continual process. What I held on to yesterday as truth could be a partial truth tomorrow. I now seek out opportunities to learn from people, books, seminars, and training. I have learnt so much since that decision in 2020 to change my mindset. I have come a long way, and I know I still have so much to learn. There are days when I revert to that old way of thinking.

But now, I just acknowledge the thought, put it back in its box, then pick myself up and let the true me show up.

My encouragement to you is to know that you can change your story, remove the mask, and be you, the real YOU.

9

HAPPY EVER AFTER? NAVIGATING MARRIAGE CRISIS

RHONDA IONIEZ

'The steps of a good man are ordered by the Lord: and he delighteth in his way.' (Psalm 37 v 23; KJV)

I embraced the Navigating Life ethos that the platform was for women to learn, share, connect, and grow. How we achieved this was entirely up to each individual in their own time, at their own pace, but with the support of like-minded women.

Enthused with this assertive vibe of inspiration and empowerment, I decided to take that audacious step and put pen to paper when the opportunity came to contribute to this anthology. This was the first step on a journey to fulfil my ambition to write a book.

Can You Imagine?

Lydia woke up, having only had a few hours of sleep preparing for her big day, something she had imagined for such a long time. The sun was shining, birds singing, and a fluttering feeling like butterflies stirred inside her stomach. Lydia was to embark on a voyage of no return, one that would change her life entirely. She looked into the mirror. Was that really her all aglow? Her dad waited patiently to escort her to the car that awaited her for the start of the journey leading to another life. "Oh dad", she exclaimed; she was leaving the parental arms of his love to be cradled by the arms of the man, to whom she believed God had joined them together—her spiritual brother and friend.

Lydia was excited as she stepped out into the radiance of the sunlight and took a sharp intake of the crispy cold winter's morning before entering the transport to her destiny. On her arrival, her heart began to beat loudly like a beaten drum, reaching its crescendo as she stood at the top of the aisle. The familiar sound of the Bridal Chorus filled the air as Lydia's gaze synchronised with the handsome gentleman in his suave attire, smiling back at her, knowing it would not be long before they were united. The sun beamed down on them with a kaleidoscope of colour, making her blink as if catapulted in time. Lydia had a foresight of what lay ahead.

The foundation of their marriage was built upon trust, love, laughter, joy, and excitement, which overcame any disappointment, anguish, sickness, heartache, pain, and trials. As the months turned to years and years to decades, they celebrated a happy family life with their children.

Then one day, it was like someone had dropped a bomb on their marriage. The force of the impact brought destruction, devastation, and pain which penetrated the core of their relationship.

Subtly, the "enemy" crept in unawares, bringing in an assembly of events to disrupt the tranquillity of the marriage. It encroached on their love, respect, fun times, romance, family time, and everything sacred to their Christian beliefs.

The words so easily uttered, for better for worse, for richer for poorer, in sickness and in health, became sorely tested. The Christ-like husband and father figure were now seemingly controlled by something more sinister, Lydia thought. Something wasn't right! The man she loved and adored now became a stranger with Dr Jekyll and Mr Hyde-like characteristics—a tyrant and dictator. She didn't know this person. The seasonal changes in her husband's behaviour reflected the mood swings that left her wondering what was happening. The summer warmth of his laughter was replaced by a dark, icy, frosty look of winter, and the fresh, new joys of spring were supplanted with the autumnal change of his countenance and venomous vocal tones. She never knew what he would say or react to at any given situation, leaving Lydia exposed to a catalogue of events, unravelling like layers of an onion, causing a sting to their relationship as it began to unfold.

His choice of clothing changed from a crisp white shirt, coordinated suit and tie, to wearing a purple T-shirt trimmed with a fringe or a T-shirt displaying what Lydia considered to be a grotesque image of a man—depicting a black Jesus with yellow piercing eyes. When her husband came home from work, she was no longer embraced by his warm welcome and the sharing of his day with her. Instead, she glanced at a silhouette of darkness slip by and retreat to a place to be alone and engage with his new acquaintances in conversation and teachings.

All family birthdays, festive holidays, anniversary celebrations abruptly came to an end and were no longer acknowledged by him. Their weekly routines were disrupted, and even accessing money for food shopping came under his control. When in the store, she was under immense pressure to hurry up and select the goods to purchase because he had to get home at a specific time. He would make his way to the checkout whether she was ready or not. He then paid for the items, and if there was anything he disapproved of, it had to be replaced or put back on the shelf. At such times, Lydia harboured the pungency of humiliation and shame because it was evident from his emotionless stare at her that this man did not care.

He declared Saturdays were Sabbath days, which brought to the family other issues and restrictions. He would not do anything on this day and expected her to do the same, not even boil a kettle.

Lydia just could not comprehend the turn of events and found herself wrestling with her thoughts and turned to the only one she knew—the Lord, her Saviour, counsellor, and confidant. Prayer and fasting were her weapons because she recognised this was a spiritual battle, one she would have to fight if she wanted to save her husband and marriage. The ambience within the home had changed drastically; there were even moments when Lydia felt the chilling atmosphere of death. This eeriness seemed to linger as her husband's dying spirit was spiralling into the clutches of a regimented force with a quest to bring about his demise. She openly and readily acknowledged that no marriage was perfect or one-sided. She believed Jesus would steer them out of the storm of confusion and danger if they stayed and didn't bale out, regardless of how rough things became. However, this meant cooperation from both parties, but at that point, Lydia felt she was bearing it for them both. Her husband was a jeopardised soul; therefore, she had to press on, irrespective of the bleak state of their marriage.

Lydia continued in her role as a wife and mother, but she refuses to follow the practices of his new beliefs. She attended and fulfilled her church duties with the children. People from church would ask about her husband's wellbeing, and many would say they were praying for him. After a while, she found herself scurrying out the church building to avoid any uncomfortable conversations. It was all too painful, and the very mention of his name was like the reopening of a wound. When she saw other couples, it reminded her of how they used to be.

She then found herself wondering how many more couples or women were hiding behind a mask, smiling on the outside but hurting on the inside? As for Lydia, she felt ashamed, embarrassed, and an utter failure.

As time went on, Lydia found herself avoiding anything she thought may provoke him. As the Bible says, *a soft answer turneth away wrath: but grievous words stir up anger* (Proverbs 15 v 1; KJV). She, however, felt frustrated because it was hurting, and some nights were as though a floodgate had opened. Her pillow was saturated with tears, and her chest aches for the one she loved but could not reach. Only God could. So, as a form of therapy and something she could perhaps refer to later, Lydia began to write her thoughts in the form of a diary. This helped for a while with the insomnia, but when she managed to sleep, the tortured meditations engulfed her, only to be awoken with a fogged memory. There appeared to be no escape from this nightmare of melancholy.

The weeks and months seemed to pass by, and the family tried to maintain a sense of normality, but it could not be hidden that "the perfect couple", as referred to by a family member, had a problem. They had started as a beautiful rosebud in a garden of love that developed to full bloom. Now, their petals were falling and fading, like their relationship, which had been infected with a parasite. It was all so bewildering for Lydia, especially as they had so often expressed their delight and excitement, discussing how they would celebrate the milestone of their marriage. Perhaps another cruise, or a spontaneous romantic excursion, something they did so many times over the years and just generally envisaged spending many happy retirement years together. Unfortunately, that dream was shattering, as now aghast; her husband would leave their home to patrol the streets with this group of men distributing leaflets dressed in his T-shirt and military boots to some unfortunate disillusioned soul. Yet, despite Lydia not knowing when he would return home, she still felt imprisoned and annoyed. Somehow, it was as if he still had a hold on her.

It was all so upsetting for Lydia as she found herself struggling because she was considered by so many—to be a strong, bold, happy, intelligent, and God-fearing woman of purpose. A fighter and an advocate for those who needed support in times when they felt weak. So, what had happened to that woman? Was it because, as though using a whip, her husband would lash out the words, *"I am the man, you abide by my rules or get out! What I say goes. I am the head of the house."* Or similar disrespecting, demoralising words that grated on her moral? Then there were times when she retaliated to his imposing views and demands. He became angry, not with a physical attack; instead, he used psychological tactics, silent taunts as his weapon because he knew that would affect her the most.

Nonetheless, the poetic inspirational verse: *a word fitly spoken is like apples of gold in pictures of silver* (Proverb 25 v 11; KJV) enlightened and comforted her spirit, and now *"every wise woman buildeth her house: but the foolish plucketh it down with her hands* (Proverb 14 v 1; KJV). With God's direction and her desire to apply wisdom, Lydia persevered.

This, at times, seemed to be rewarded with a sense of peace and unity within the home, albeit not for long.

As if competing for more dominance, her husband flaunted the bellowing and chanting of his new doctrinal teachings. Lydia would counter it by singing Christian songs with a passion while asking the Lord to receive her praises as a fragrance of her love.

Now, she was faced with an ultimatum. Follow her husband and denounce the God she was serving to save her marriage or keep trusting God that things would change.

Lydia felt helpless but not hopeless, as the words from the Bible echoed in her mind, *"Whom shall ye serve?"* She felt torn as if mesmerised by the two-forked tongue of a cobra, sensing her vulnerability. She faced the dilemma, the love of a tangible man or the love of an invisible God. But for Lydia, there was no contest, as she snapped out of the beguiling spell of the serpent. She stated, *"You may have captured Eve, Satan, but certainly not me."* Lydia vehemently declared!

She now accepted this as part of her journey, and wherever God would lead, she would go.

Lydia always encouraged her children to still have a good relationship with their father. Her prayers and hope were that they would not be influenced by their fathers' beliefs but remain committed to their Christian faith. Thankfully, this is still the case as they develop their own relationship with God.

Forgiveness for Lydia didn't come easily; the thoughts of the past, verbal abuse, and ridicule had left their emotional marks. But over time, through prayer, devotion, and trusting that God was in complete control of her life, she found the courage, tenacity, and resilience she needed to stay in her marriage.

So, with a renewed confidence, Lydia proclaimed:

"Yes, I have been disrespected as a wife, mother, and woman, but I am the head and not the tail. I will not be trampled by anything or anyone. I will hold my head up high, for God loves me unconditionally. I am an overcomer. I will stand my ground, for *'I am my beloved's, and my beloved is mine'* (Songs of Solomon 6 v 3; NKJV). This is not the end, but my beginning."

No one knows what lies ahead on this journey of life, but whatsoever I am going through, I must take one day at a time. I should not bring "tomorrows" problem into my today. After all, tomorrow is not promised!

As for those I love, let them know they're loved. Take nothing and no one for granted. I must make time for myself, and most of all, LOVE MYSELF!

With that positive notion, the familiar tune, the Bridal Chorus by Wagner, sounded in the distance. The twinkling sun beamed, and Lydia blinked, then as if propelled back to the present, Lydia smiled; she was getting married. I wonder what the future holds!

(Songs of Solomon 8 v 7; KJV: *'Many waters cannot quench love, neither can the floods drown it'*)

Can you imagine?

10

FROM ABUSE TO SELF LOVE: NAVIGATING BAD RELATIONSHIPS

CLAUDETTE SAMUEL

I was born on the 20th of March 1961 in Kingston Town, Jamaica, Halfway Tree, to be exact. My mother is Victoria Davis, and my father was unknown, as recorded on my birth certificate. I never spoke with my mother about who my father was, and to be honest, I was not curious and was happy with the dad I had. My mother was 26 years old when she gave birth to me, and she already had a child, my brother, who was two and a half years old. We lived with other family members in Jamaica until my grandmother sent for us to live in the UK. I was eight months old when I left Jamaica. There was a story told to me by my late uncle, who we called uncle Papa. He always said I was his souvenir. He said if it were not for my mother being pregnant with me, he might have still been in Jamaica. You see, he was able to travel on the ticket meant for my mum. I believe that everything was for a reason then, and everything is for a reason now.

Growing Up In The UK

I felt I had a privileged upbringing compared to some of my friends who did not have both parents. My stepdad was not my biological father, but to me, he was. He brought me up, and he was the only father figure I knew. I will always be grateful that he was man enough to take on another man's children, as he adopted my brother and me. I was the only girl out of four children that my mother had, which gave me some extra privileges. I found out in my later years that my dad did have a daughter who passed away as a baby, so I guess for my dad, I was his little girl.

I spent my childhood years mainly in Hackney. I could almost say I was born and bred there, but it was pretty much the only place I knew that I could call home. I went to Gayhurst Primary School and later attended Shoreditch Secondary School. I could be talkative one moment and then quiet the next. You had to get to know me to appreciate the qualities I had. I was a sensitive person and felt deeply about things.

I was very self-conscious about my body. I felt like plain Jane, as most of the time growing up, I would look like a boy more than a girl. I was not your typical girl who wore pink dresses and bows in her hair. It was hard to be girly, having three brothers. I was a tomboy through and through and loved to play with the boys on my road. I liked to play rough, and I would do all the things that boys would. I felt I had something to prove; I could do anything they could. I was competitive, which may have been why I was sporty. I was a sprinter and was good at most sports. As I got older, my body began to develop, and I embraced the new me. I was still unhappy with some of my body parts, as most young ladies are. There would always be something displeasing that they wanted to change. For me, it was my teeth—the mottling on my teeth was the worst part of me. I hated it the most. This was not caused by decay or eating sweets. I later learnt the reason for it when my daughter developed the same condition. When her adult teeth came through, I was told it was dental fluorosis. I tried hard for her not to have the same problem, but she did. It was my effort to avoid it that made it worse as I would brush her teeth often and allow her to have her toothbrush, which she would keep in her mouth. I know now that there is no shame in this, but for me, it was. I would have liked white and perfectly formed teeth. I also had some crooked teeth, and as a tomboy, it did not really matter, but as a girl, it did.

The Boyfriend

I was now at the age where boys took an interest in girls. I was no longer the tomboy I used to be. However, the boys in my school who I would hang out with were friends, and the older ones were like brothers to me, as they respected the girls in school and were very protective of them. I tried telling this to my dad, who would often see me walking down the road in a group. I know, it probably did not look great, but really, it was no big deal. If I ever wanted to go to Friday club, where the youth would hang out on a Friday evening, I would need to sneak out as I was not allowed to be out late. This was always exciting, as I would find all different ways of going out and coming in. The front door was an option I would rarely use.

My problem was that I had just as many friends that were boys as I had girlfriends. These teen years became difficult for me, and I suppose for my dad too, as I was growing up and was not quite his little girl anymore (albeit a tomboy), which he recognised.

I quickly transitioned from tomboy/girl child to teenager and gradually moved into deep waters of womanhood, which came with all its feelings and emotions that were sometimes hard to understand. I liked boys but found I now liked boys in a different way. I became involved with a teenage boy two years my senior. He had already left school. He'd often show up outside of my school to meet with friends. We soon became friends, and then over time, we became an item. He was a charmer; he was known as Apache to those who knew him well, as he had long straight black hair. His parents were of Caribbean-Indian descent.

It was the days of sound systems, and he was part of one, so going out was a regular thing. I supported the sound system and would go wherever they were playing. I became unruly; I disobeyed my parents and stayed out late, even all night, not returning home. I was doing what I wanted to do. I thought I was happy with the life that I was leading as a teenager; however, it put a strain on my relationship with my family and even some of my friends, as I spent more time with my boyfriend than I did with them. I soon became a statistic, young girl, pregnant! I miscarried but became pregnant again the second time. As my boyfriend was not interested in becoming a father, I had a termination, and I did not want to be a single teenage mother with no prospects.

My life pretty much was going downhill from there—my parents, family, and boyfriend seemed to have had enough of me. I was an embarrassment, a let-down. I felt very much like an outsider and felt alone and unloved by those closest to me. I realised that my boyfriend was not really for me, in the same way I was for him. This really became apparent when I needed him the most, when I had nowhere to go. He ignored me when I was pregnant; he did not want to know. He left the decision for me to make alone. I was just a trophy to him, and now I was a tarnished one. I should have realised way before then that the way I was being treated was not normal, or should I say, 'a loving relationship.' He used to beat me when he thought that I was being unfaithful to him, which was not the case. He was the jealous type, and if anyone looked at me, it was my fault. This would happen quite often as going out and being part of the sound system follower made me vulnerable to this type of behavior. I put up with this bad behavior because I thought I loved him, and he loved me too, and this was his way of showing it. He would always apologise and be loving towards me after beating me; that's what always made me go back. He was tender and genuinely appeared remorseful.

From Dream To Nightmare

Experiencing this relationship was the one that made me uncompromising in future relationships. It also made me a little hardened in my approach to any new relationships. It certainly made me strong enough to be able to say no to anyone else putting their hand on me. It was my teacher that helped me when no one else would. I did eventually move around from one family member to another while I was trying to find my way back into the lives of my family and friends. I was tainted, or at least, I felt that way.

It took me a while to get back into a place of control and self-worth; however, I prolonged going into another relationship. When I did, we started as friends. He was someone I could talk to; we both had good jobs, so we talked about buying a home together. Things seemed to be looking up for me. We were together a little while before I became pregnant. I felt ready this time to be a mother. I spent a couple of years in the relationship after having my daughter, but again, the relationship became abusive, and I nipped it in the bud very quickly.

I went away to Marseille for a break to think about what I needed to do, and I came back with my game plan. I showed my daughter's father the door; he tried the ring trick and asked me to marry him. I said yes at first; I think it was what I wanted to hear at the time. I wanted to be a married woman with a husband, a family, and a home. Is that not what most women want out of life? Some call it the dream? For me, it would have been a nightmare. As soon as I said yes, I quickly came to my senses and said no. He was mad at my change of response. I later found out he was not only a beater but a cheater; I suppose it goes hand in hand! For me, it was good riddance to bad rubbish. I knew I was worth more than that. I guess I had a fortunate escape. This was not my destiny, nor was it my portion.

When I'd had enough after going into another relationship that was not violent this time, I still felt worthless, used, and humiliated. I still was not the queen I was destined to be, and not for the lack of trying. I thought this was the man that would be my king; he was already the father of my twins after a relationship of 11 years. I struggled with who I was, what I wanted, and where I wanted to be.

Turning A Corner

I did not want unhealthy relationships to define me, as that was not who I wanted to be—a victim of abuse, an object to be used, a trophy to be added to a collection of other trophies. That was not me! I did, however, feel that all my relationships had left some indelible marks, not physical ones, thankfully, but more emotional. It has made me stronger as a woman, a queen accepting nothing less than a king.

I've not traveled this journey on my own; I know that God has been with me all the way and has faithfully kept me through all my dark moments. There has been many, particularly as my last relationship of many years, I have not penned yet. A lack of a king in my life is not the end of my story. I have achieved many things along the way. I have become a queen with my own kingdom; that's the king(dom) in me.

My journey so far has been rocky at times; however, I would not change a thing, as throughout this, God's hand has been on my life. It has made me resilient and strong, and I am starting to live in my purpose. It has taken me all my adult years to this point to realise how beautiful I am, and despite the parts of me that I disliked, God loves them and loves me. I am okay with who I am, as I affirm myself daily.

I look back and think of my mother, my grandmother, who I called Gran, and other women in my family, who have had to work extremely hard to be the best they could be. First and foremost, for themselves and their children, who didn't allow them to be mistreated or used as an object of gratification for men. My Gran's personal story as to why she was single when she came to the UK, I do not know. I do know that my maternal grandfather was in my mother's life, long enough for me to know him from a young age. I believe that my Gran's fight to do better was born out of sheer determination, and it was for her children and her grandchildren. She did not focus on the lack of support (of a husband) to provide for her family. The legacy that my Gran left was huge. Out of this woman and the women before her, they have all brought forth strong woman, of which I am one. I know where my Gran's strength came from as she was a God-fearing woman, a virtuous one at that.

What I have experienced and observed over the years is that some women have a weak spot for jokers. I would describe it as a downtrodden mindset, where they settle for less than what they deserve. They believe they are not good enough to find and keep a true king. Or is it that women are too strong-willed and strong-minded, and that may have driven the right person away? My story is this story, but I have chosen to accept my singleness as I find myself and define who I am. The Christ in me tells me that I have a king who is preparing for his queen. The role of kings and their attributes are important to me, even at this stage of my life. I am not looking to find a king, but I will say, if it is God's will, bring him and let me see.

I have chosen to rise out of my situation by submitting to God's will for my life and accept what He has in store for me. Sometimes, it feels like time has been wasted, but the truth is, I have been through all to be refined and prepared for a time like now. There is so much available to me to learn and grow, and I can work on myself to be the best that I can be.

I could have given up many times, but I did not. My born-again journey restarted as a result of seeking love that I could not find.

I have overcome being used and abused by those who say they loved me. There is a song about finding love in all the wrong places; that was my song back then.

Today, I am proud to be the mother of three amazing daughters who are all striving to be the best that they can be and what God wants them to be—a queen with a king and a kingdom of their own.

I am today, a no-nonsense, strong-minded, free-willed, loving, and caring person—a balanced mix of soft and hard, not necessarily in that order. My dialogue is straight-talking and plain. I tell it as it is and believe the good, bad, and ugly parts have blended to make me who I am. I know that if it were not for God on my side, I could be in an abusive relationship or worse. I have been freed from the life I was living because Jesus loves me!

11

MISSIONARY WINNIFRED THOMAS: NAVIGATING A LIFE OF SERVICE

DAWN THOMAS WALLACE

This is the story of my mother, Winnifred Donaldson. She was born on the 13th of July 1936, the eighth of nine children. She was beautiful, and from a young age, it was clear she was incredibly intelligent. As a result, she was sent to school early. Her family were primarily landowners and she enjoyed a comfortable life in Douce, Clarendon, Jamaica. Ever a vibrant storyteller, Mum often told us of her own mother making food parcels and giving them to children, as they passed the family home; to take to their mothers after shopping at the village shop. Taking in her mother's image, Mum was a beautiful child, and from a young age it was clear she was incredibly intelligent. As a result, she was sent to school early.

At the age of six, Mum moved to Ocho Rios, St Anne, to live with her mother's cousin, Mr McKenzie "Papa" (a pharmacy dispenser) and his wife - themselves substantial property owners – together with her eldest sister, Aunt Lou. There, she enjoyed a pleasant and luxurious life; free from want. She had her own chauffeur to take her to and from school as well as maids; she lived in palatial surroundings. Mum attended an Anglican church, where her family were assigned special named seating. Hers was the life of a princess, so much as that when British royalty arrived in Jamaica, Mum was headhunted to provide premium service; she attended Princess Alice, Countess of Athlone, on her stays in Jamaica while performing duties as Chancellor of the University College of the West Indies. Extravagance, however, was never necessarily the definition of satisfaction; Mum yearned for more, for her soul, and longed to be back with her parents and siblings.

One day, her curious footsteps were passing by a Pentecostal church when she overheard the joyful singing. Pulled by the infectious sound, her heart warmed as she drew near listening intently to the powerful worship and fiery sermon. Before long, she was spotted and word had reached her adoptive mother. On arrival home, she was reprimanded and warned not to have any association with "those Pentecostals" who were deemed beneath their standards. Poor people. But Mum knew they had something her spirit agonised for.

Nearing seventeen, her pining for her mother prevailed and she returned to Clarendon. Shortly after, she fully surrendered her life to Christ, became a committed Christian and attended a Pentecostal Church led by Bishop W. A. Shaw.

Mum moved to Kingston to study and lived with her good friends – the Giscombe Family. As a student, Mum experienced hardship; something she had never been privy to before. She, however, never disclosed this to her parents in Clarendon; fearing they would question why she was suffering hardship when prior to becoming a devout Christian she lacked nothing and enjoyed the wealth of the world. Without doubt, God proved faithful and supplied her every need.

In 1962, Mum moved to England. It was wonderful to be reunited with two of her brothers (who sponsored her) and she resided with Uncle P in Northampton. Nethertheless, she missed meeting with other Christians. There were no lively churches around and she felt as though she could not endure it any longer. Mum wrote to her good friend Rev. Daphne Crossfield (whom she fondly called "D" and who in turn called her "P") instructing, "Get me a room." It was not long before Mum could enjoy fellowship with believers in London.

Whilst Mum was worshipping, Ulric Tivius Thomas (Dad) was smitten by her breath-taking looks. His eyes gazed at this beautiful Christian lady and desired her in marriage. In those days, marriage had to be sought through the Pastor and Senior Officers of the Church. Mum prayed about it, but she also had to get permission from her eldest brother, Percy – who was not a Christian at the time. Uncle Percy was not impressed. He could not understand how Mum wanted to get married so quickly after arriving in the country; claiming "God gave me a vision." It took the smoking of a long cigarette before he could give her the go-ahead.

On Saturday 8th September 1962, our parents were married. Two beautiful, loving and caring families (the Thomases and Donaldsons) were joined, remaining together to this day. This union produced four children: Winsome, Anthony, Samuel and Dawn. Mum and Dad experienced many highs and many lows – healings, victories, rejection and racism. Often Mum was ill, and Dad was the only breadwinner. In every situation, God supplied all their needs to the point they were able to help many others.

Together, they served in the church from the 1960s to 2020. Their greatest gifting was hospitality and their home provided shelter to many missionaries throughout the world – the Caribbean, Africa, India, Canada, United States of America, Europe and Indonesia. This was Mum's joy – her niche; and she excelled at it. Mum made no distinction between people. She simply loved them. They were all the same in her eyes; whichever background they came from. Being of mixed racial origin, Mum was uniquely placed to communicate with people from all walks of life – rich or poor, diverse racial backgrounds, gender, age, gay or straight. Her father was half Scottish, her mother half Indian with a Mongolian mix and to add to all of this Mum was a Jewish descendant (we learned this from our Uncle P in one of his many family history sessions we were privy to; tracing back four generations), hence her distinctive features.

She saw individuals' souls. Somehow when people left her presence they left with the feeling of a full heart and a spark of light twinkled within them. Moving to the church in Slough, she was clear on her mission and purpose; declaring God had told her she was called to gather the remnants of His people. That was certainly true. Mum and Dad had their work cut out for them. Many families were suffering and their job was to soothe their wounds, heal and restore them.

During the 1980s, one of Mum's colleagues named Bernard (a young Irish man) suffered with AIDS. At the time, this was a taboo subject and many Christians passed judgement. Not Mum. Bernard became very ill and was rejected by all – especially those he had called friends. Mum heard the slander and hypocrisy of others and stood against it. She strode to where Bernard lived and knocked on the door. He refused to answer because of fear of the hatred of others. Mum stood firm and refused to leave. Sheepishly, he opened the door, begging her to stay away from him lest she caught his disease. Mum, nonetheless, warmly embraced him, fed him and washed his clothes. Whilst dying, he called for one person: "Mrs Thomas". This is an example of the count-less people Mum affectionately helped over decades of faithful service.

Mum was a defender of the weak. She feared no one; only God. When members of the church fell into finan-cial difficulties and were about to have their homes repossessed her response was always, "Not on my watch!" She would prayerfully seek God for a strategy to solve their problems and, armed with a plan, would arrange meetings with bank managers and make her proposals. Sometimes, they were fierce and determined to throw members out of their homes, but somehow there was always a shift in mindset and Mum's requests were granted. I even witnessed a salesman reduced to tears begging Mum to not speak anymore. A power radiated through her. Mum never attended meetings unarmed. She was always mounted up in prayer and faith in God. He intervened at every stage and she *always* gained the victory. Some of the individuals she helped are today great-grandparents still living in their homes.

These skills proved crucial for the purchase of Faith Temple Church (Slough). Mum was in the frontline of the negotiations and both our parents were happy to put their home up for guarantee to purchase the church building. Mum was loved and respected by ministers from various Christian organisations and members from a wide variety of religious faiths. It was clear she was a great communicator. She stood for justice, told the truth and counselled many ministers. She was a rock to our father and her children.

One of Mum's favourite programmes was Judge Judy, which she watched religiously no less than three hours every day. Likewise, she counselled myriads of people and was a lifeline to multitudinous families. Even where parents had given up on their children, Mum still believed in them, gave them hope and provided care and shelter. Those suffering from domestic violence found a safe haven in our home.

Mum was indeed a fabulous cook, but she was so much more than that. Our house was always full. Our parents never regarded their belongings so dear to them that they would forsake the needy. All were welcome. She served church conventions, her Pension Club, the community and organised Missionaries' Dinners (which also brought couples together in marriage). Thus, our kitchen needed refurbishing repeatedly with wear and tear. Our parents allowed their home to be broken down, so that they could mend the lives of others'. With old age, being retired and ill health Mum was unable to refurbish her kitchen as quickly as she would have liked, but it remained a focus for her. It was her urgent dying wish to give her kitchen a final makeover. When I had outlined the plans to her and confirmed the date the building work would commence, she laid her head on her pillow and sighed, "Thank God." Mum held on to see the work commence. In fact, on the day the renovation had started Mum passed away.

Although our Mother helped countless families, she never took her eye off the ball. Whilst caring for others she remembered her own; supporting the care of her own Mother (who lived until the age of 100 years) together with a few of her siblings, Mum would tell us that she had four children and she studied each of them. She knew how to wisely deal with us.

Mum was straight talking. She was not afraid to stamp out wrong or face dangerous situations. She would blast your head off and then turn around and be so friendly, as if nothing had happened. She was very forgiving and always told you the truth. On one occasion, a gossiper thought it necessary to tell her about the misdemeanour of certain individuals. Mum's response came forth like cold rain. She calmly said, *"Well, let's deal with the demons in you first. Then, we'll go over and sort out those people."* Needless to say, that gossiper never came back.

On another occasion, during one of our evening services, a tall drunkard staggered into the church shouting and mocking. "Hallelujah!" he would bellow frequently. Everyone in the church was agitated and desperate for him to leave, but no one did anything about it. No one, except Mum. She boldly marched down the aisle, faced the Brobdingnagian - who towered over her - with angry eyes as her shield and sword (Mum spoke with her eyes). Pointing her finger towards the door, Mum commanded with authority, "Come out!" The monstrous and violent figure's jaw gaped open. Feared gripped him by the throat. Without hesitation, he scampered through the door like an overgrown puppy.

Mum saw money as a tool: not to be loved, but to be used to do great good. How she loved her £50 notes; anything less was too small for her! Even during her illness, Mum continued to hold pardners. Such an amazing woman!

Sadly, in 2017 Mum was diagnosed with breast cancer. Throughout the illness, Mum remained strong in faith and always worshipped. She suffered greatly and was in considerable pain. Despite this, she never complained. Instead, she would say, *"What's the use? Just give God thanks."* Throughout this journey, Mum continued coun-selling, praying and providing for those in need and always wore the most elaborate outfits. Going to the hospital for treatment was another occasion to dress up; she was an icon.

On Tuesday 3rd November 2020, Mum was promoted to glory. As death approached, it was like she had seen or heard something out of the ordinary. Something supernatural. There was an urgency, as if someone was coming for her. There was an urgency as if something, or someone, was coming for her. She knew she had to be prepared and desired to sit up in readiness. "Lift up my head," she urged. As I tried to lift up my Mother's head, she instructed me further. "Put your hand behind my neck." I followed my Mother's instructions, eager to please and adhere to her wishes. Once Mum was in the desired position she peacefully passed away.

I am not sure what Mum saw – was it sweet heavenly chariots or our Saviour Himself? One thing I do know: she was prepared and ready to meet Him.

The lessons we learn from my mother's legacy are the importance of living to please God; by being genuine and transparent. Kindness and a lifestyle of charitable giving (using the resources you have been blessed with – however small) enables you to touch the lives of many beyond your borders. The more you give; the more you have to give. God's resources are limitless, and He is willing and ready to empower those who surrender to His will. By being a shining light in a very dark and cold world, sharing and caring for others, we fulfil the great commission of our Saviour.

12

POWER OF FORGIVING FAMILY: NAVIGATING FORGIVENESS

LILIAN WANGARI

It is the last day of the semester, the last module of the course. I am excited not only because I will be having two weeks break, but I will also be a term away from completing my diploma in Special Needs Education. Looking back, I cannot but marvel at how far I have come from and the sacrifices I have had to make to come this far, including working extra hours to fund my education. To say I am excited is an understatement. At last, there seems to be some light at the end of the tunnel. My hard work is about to show; my sacrifices are about to pay off; my dream of promotion and eventually a better pay seems to be just a step away. I am delighted. Not long before enrolling in this course, I had secured a job as a Teaching Assistant at a British international school. This was after a long wait, having completed another diploma in Early Childhood Education and staying jobless for quite a while. I am happy, earning decent pay, in a good working environment, living by myself, and having just that little freedom that is every young woman's dream.

During this period, I met the love of my life, got married, and moved to the United Kingdom, and later I was blessed with two children. But life had not always been like this.

Kenya

I was born in one of the slums in Kenya, a country in the eastern part of Africa as an only child to a teenage single mum. Life was not perfect, but my mum made sure that she gave her all to provide the basic needs for me, despite being young and quite vulnerable herself. She would visit the neighbouring country, buy clothes, and sell them back home. Words would never be enough to describe how amazing and hardworking my mother was. She was incredibly kind, brave, and generous. I grew up loved, cared for, and she always assured me that I mattered and was important to her, especially as her only child. Though sometimes things were difficult, with business not doing well, my mum always reminded me that God was the centre of our lives. I spent most evenings reading the Bible, singing hymns, and reciting memory verses with her. My early years in primary school were remarkable; I excelled in my studies. I was a top-three student throughout my primary school years.

On the other hand, my mum's business was not doing so well as laws and regulations of entering the neighbouring countries got tightened with every new government regime. I sat for my end-year exams and passed exceptionally well. However, my joy would be short-lived when

I realised that it would be impossible to join a boarding school that I had been offered a placement.

At that moment, I understood there were two options: either drop out of school completely or go back and repeat the last year of primary school. I chose the latter; it was tough to see my former classmates and friends, some who had not even performed as well as I had, join different schools countrywide. Honestly, that following year was stressful. I developed very low self-esteem. I was no longer the confident girl I used to be. I was engulfed with fear of the unknown because I knew inside me, there was a possibility that I may never join secondary school.

The year went on quickly, and I sat for the exams yet again. This time to my shock, I performed much better than before and was lucky to get placement to an even better boarding school than before. Once again, my mum was unable to raise the full expected amount. That broke my heart. With the little savings that she got, we decided that as an alternative, it was best if I went to a day school because it had less expenses.

Along with my good grades, it was not going to be difficult to find one, so we embarked on a mission to look, hoping and praying for the best. I was so elated when my mum came home one day, weeks later, and told me she found a school for me. It was the best news I had received in a while. I had waited for this moment for too long and was glad it was here.

When I joined the new school, it was already a month into the term, and learning had begun, but I wasn't discouraged. I settled in well, made friends, and tried as much as I could to catch up with what I had missed. It was going all well until about two years later when my mum started experiencing health issues. It first began with a fever one day, then a severe headache the following day, then there were mixed symptoms that kept changing by the day. Several visits to the doctors revealed nothing serious, and she was sent back home with pain killers. We visited numerous local hospitals, but the story remained the same, and without proper medical cover, it was difficult to get a proper diagnosis for her. All we held on to were prayers.

At the beginning of the third year, it was evident that I would have to drop out of school for lack of school fees and take care of my mum. It was painful for both of us, but to get her back on her feet was all that mattered. I remained at home, and though I thought there would be a miracle, two out of the three school terms found me still at home. It was during these lonely and dark times and in total desperation, that for the first time, the idea to find my biological father came alive. I had some basic information from a conversation I previously had with mum. This is what I would use to piece together where he might be and secretly locate him.

The day finally came, and I met my dad for the first time after spending days doing my research. It was an awkward moment. Firstly, I was filled with guilt and shame for not telling my mum. I knew it was going to break her heart. Secondly, having gone through a rough time, my expectations were great. I was ill-prepared in terms of how I was going to deal with any negative response. He was, for obvious reasons, shocked. Our first conversation was very uncomfortable, coupled with long moments of silence, but I ultimately found the courage to explain to him my reason for wanting to meet.

I told him about the predicament my mum was in. He listened and promised to sort me out as far as my education was concerned. He even asked me to give him the fee structure on my next visit. To me, this was like a dream come true. I was so happy I almost forgot that he had never been a part of my life until now.

Soon, I realised this would be the start of so many other trips filled with lots of tears, disappointments, and empty promises. Many times, he stood me up after waiting for him for hours. Each visit was hurting, but I was desperate to complete school, so I kept going back. I was also young, barely fifteen years old, naïve, but determined. I could not think of any other way. It was now nearly a year since I was last in school. I missed it; I missed my friends, and so when I receive a message from the headteacher to report back to school to sit for the end of year exams, my joy knew no bounds. These exams were going to determine if I was going to join the last year of secondary. Miraculously, I passed, which meant if I could raise the fees the following year, I would be allowed to sit for my final year examination.

The last year of school was traumatic. I was in and out of school till I completed it. As I expected, I did not do well. I was devastated, but I knew with time, that I would be able to join a college. Life outside the school was equally tough. I had to get a job to assist my mum, and so when a friend introduced me to a company that was advertising a hawking job as a 'sales' job, I was up for it. We would pitch merchandises in the streets, offices, and traffic jams all day. It was a tricky business as we risked being arrested because it was illegal to hawk in the streets without a license. About a year into it, I quit when I got another opportunity to work in a hotel. The working hours were crazy, and the pay was low, but it was safer than being out hawking in the streets with the risk of being arrested.

Back home, my mum was in and out of the hospital. Sometimes, she seemed fine, and other times, she would be bedridden. All this time, there was never a clear diagnosis of what she was suffering from. As if this were not enough, she was battling a court case between her and her brothers involving a piece of land that had been left to her by her late father. This became a relentless battle that left her weak physically, emotionally, and spiritually. In desperation once again, I decided to approach my dad just one more time, hoping that he could take me to college. All I wanted was to be in school and follow my dreams. Once again, it became like a game of cat and mouse.

One day, he finally told me that it was best if I did not bother him anymore. My heart was shattered. I sat by the side of the road and cried as I watched him walk away from me literally, and that was the last time I saw him. I was hit with a feeling of rejection, abandonment, and betrayal. What hurts the most were the lies.

I never told anyone I had contacted him, and there was no way I was going to tell my mum. So, I had to carry the hurt and pain I felt alone.

My mum's health continued to be a challenge. One morning, coming home from a night shift, I found her extremely weak but strangely very jovial. I decided it was best if we rushed her to the hospital. I quickly arranged with a relative of hers and a friend to accompany her while I remained behind to freshen up and join them in the hospital on my way to a night shift. After holding hands and praying together, they left. This was to become one of the most regrettable decisions of my life. As soon as they left, my heart was filled with so much sadness. I sat on the sofa to pray; the next thing I heard was a loud knock on the door. When I opened my eyes and instantly checked the wall clock, I had been asleep for well over four hours. The moment I opened the door, I saw the two ladies standing in front of the door, one holding the slippers my mum wore when she left that morning. I did not need to be told.

At the young age of forty, with so much life ahead of her, my mum was no more. As I laid on the sofa, tired and broken, my mum breathed her last. How was I ever going to forgive myself? Where would I start? How would I live without her? Who would encourage and cheer me on? At that very moment, I just wanted to join her.

The days ahead were tough for me; it was up to me to make the necessary funeral arrangements. Mum's relatives made no or minimal effort to participate, probably because of the disagreement and the court battles. One incident that broke me so much was a day after my mum's death, we were informed that there was a mix-up. The identification number we were given at the hospital did not match the body that was received at the morgue. Therefore, they needed someone to go and manually search amongst the bodies that had been brought in that day and the previous day.

I remember I literally begged some of my relatives to do this as it was going to be very tough for me, but they gave me all manner of excuses. It was two of my friends that assisted me in searching for my mum amongst all the bodies. It was so painful. As difficult as things were, friends, neighbours, co-workers, and I worked tirelessly day and night to put together all that was needed to bury my mum. My young mind could not comprehend why so much was happening to me. Several days later, everything came all together, and we were able to give my mum a befitting burial ceremony. It was one of the most difficult days of my life. I miss my mum terribly, but it is a different kind of missing. My heart is not filled with painful thoughts of guilt or shame of having not shared with her that one secret. It is filled with the peace of knowing that my intentions were right. There has never been a day that ever passed without me thinking of her. I see her in everything good in life. I no longer grieve with sadness, as my heart is full of gratitude for the wonderful years we shared, and for the love and sacrifices she made for me. I know she is in a better place.

With my mum gone and with no stable source of income, I knew things were going to get harder. As if that were not enough, I lost the only job I had.

New Beginnings

Some months later, by God's grace, a friend I went to high school with had since relocated to the UK. They invited me to stay with their family, and while I was there, I joined a college where I studied Early Childhood Education. I passed the course and eventually, after a long search, secured a job.

People have different ways of dealing with pain. I hid mine in a smile. It was difficult for people around me to comprehend the amount of pain I was carrying. It was anger, grief, bitterness, and sadness that I held inside. I had refused to let go, and not even the great sermons I listened to or great books I read could ease my misery.

The way I was feeling began to affect every aspect of my life, including my work, my relationships with friends, and even my dating life. My pain was real.

I recognised that I had to make a conscious decision to let go of the anger, resentment, and retribution that I had towards those who I believed betrayed, abandoned, and rejected me. Not dealing with these issues was hindering me from moving forward in life. I felt like time for me had stopped at the exact moment all the pain occurred, and I couldn't move past it. I had to intentionally restart the clock of my life and keep it moving.

The journey through forgiveness was difficult and very personal, but in the end, liberating and rewarding. To know that forgiveness has nothing to do with the other person but has everything to do with me was so freeing.

Most importantly, I discovered that there would be no way to begin this journey without first reconciling and admitting to my past failures and imperfections. I knew I had to forgive myself first before I could extend the same to others. The Book of Mathew chapter 6:14-15, in the Bible, is a perfect reminder that forgiveness works two ways.

Matthew 6:14-15 (NIV)

For if you forgive other people when they sin against you, your heavenly Father will also forgive you. But if you do not forgive others their sins, your Father will not forgive your sins.

You cannot ask God to forgive you and fail to extend the same to others. To continue holding on to the past would only mean forgetting that I am also a product of God's grace. I am alive today because of His love, goodness, and mercy. He forgives me every time, even when I do not deserve it. As a Christian, I believe that forgiveness is a step of obedience as God commands us. We do not have to wait to feel 'ready' to let go, because more often, emotions follow actions. Therefore, when I acted submissively by letting it go, I knew how to trust that the emotions will come one day. It was helpful to discover that the main reason for forgiveness is not necessarily for reconciliation, but so I can move on. Nor does it mean that I condone the wrongs people have done, but I recognise that God is the only One who can truly judge another.

Forgiveness enabled me to be free and taught me to have boundaries in my life, to protect my space, and guard my heart. I thank God that I entered marriage after I had walked through my journey of forgiveness, as this has enabled me to navigate through issues wisely as a wife, mother, and all my relationships.

I am more sensitive in how I treat other people, and I am quick to settle matters before they get out of control. Also, I have taught myself to walk away from situations and relationships that are likely to inflict pain on my loved ones or me. I want to stay in an environment that my children can thrive in a positive setting by God's grace. This would have been impossible if I were still holding onto my past. Letting go gave me a fresh start.

13

FINDING LOVE THAT HEALS: NAVIGATING ABUSE

CHARLENE BROWN

I recall growing up in church from around the age of eight, often looking for ways to avoid attending Sunday school. With most Sundays, I scrambled my brain to devise what I believed to be an ingenious plan to induce my parents. On the Sundays that I succeeded, my lips curled around my face, pleased that I could spend the day as I wanted, but the reminders to maintain the charade stayed close. Another Sunday would depend on it, and even if it didn't, the exposure of the lie wouldn't be worth being beaten for. They say all good things come to an end, and despite my protests, I realised that the fight just wasn't worth it. Even with my sullen face, I was sternly told that I needed to fix it, and I quickly learned that the voice of a child was not loud enough to dictate the decision of her parents, and over time, I came to appreciate the place that would save me. It also became my second home.

As a child growing up, confidence didn't walk hand in hand with me and carrying excess pounds didn't help. Losing weight welcomed male attention, especially outside the confines of the church and whilst I acknowledged this, I was conscious that I didn't want to incite more than I could handle. I had seen and heard enough stories of young people who had 'fallen' and either never returned or made the decision to remain at church but were relegated to the backbench. I wasn't a girl who welcomed attention or shame, but neither did I want to stray away from the place I knew as my extended family.

It Never Was Love

I was in my early twenties when I met him. Somehow, I had managed to receive an invite to a private function from my friends who had not too long ago met him. From his heavy Caribbean accent, it was apparent that he had not been in the country for long. His dialect was raw and sporadically injected with language that wasn't suited for sensitive ears; nevertheless, he held the attention of those who sat at his table. I understood why my friend insisted that I meet him, and although I believe he was conscious of who God was, he managed to tread a fine line.

I had heard many words from the church pulpit warning people against being "unequally yoked", but now that I sat opposite him, those words faded slightly, and I found myself being drawn to his humour and charm. I wasn't oblivious to the fact that we lived in two different worlds, but with him came an air of excitement accompanied by a promise of something I had never known before. I don't know if the words about the danger of playing with fire had been amplified in my head, but if I did, I played anyway. I had seen enough to know that he was confident to draw women to him, but he was not a gentleman. Maybe I allowed myself to believe that I could dance with him on the periphery and leave the relationship unscathed. He invited me to the centre stage, and I was swayed.

To the outside world, I fought hard against the projection of the truth because its exposure would smear me with the heart-wrenching decision of walking away and right now, I wasn't willing to do that. It was easier to say that we were only talking. And from where I was standing, that wasn't a sin.

In-between the laughter and the excitement that my new-found love gave me, it was only a matter of time before the cajoling for intimacy came. I was familiar with the words written on the pages of the Bible, but I had already allowed myself to be swept along my new-found journey, and despite my resolve not to, I surrendered to my weakness. I told myself that I was with a man who loved me and wanted him to know that I felt the same.

I remember hearing that the first time should be something special but what he had given in exchange was far from that. I imagined something slow and intimate, but what I got back felt emotionless and painful, and I just wanted him to finish quickly. My mind anxiously flitted between the discharge that would stain his mother's bedsheet and where I now found myself. For a man who always had something to say, it was clear that he was disappointed that I didn't bleed and asked more than once if it had been my first time.

I believe that this was my first wound, and although the reality hit me, I could not afford to let the sting of it linger over me. No doubt, the next time would be different. Perhaps he couldn't have spent the time that he really wanted, given his family members were in the house at the time, and any interruption would have yielded an embarrassment, perhaps not so much to him but certainly to me. But even though I fought to dismiss what had physically happened, it was harder to ignore the gnawing that had started crawling in my soul.

Apart from my closest friends, it was less complicated to tell everyone that he was just a friend, but even with that, I began to feel like there were 'eyes' watching me. I was conscious that my words often betrayed me, but I also knew that even when I managed to navigate myself through the lie, I could not hide from the God who sees everything, even though I silently hoped that He didn't.

I knew that opening the depths of the pain I worked so hard to hide would only invite shame. Although I had suppressed much of what I had seen and felt, the truth stung, while the place that I had stuffed the pain was filling quickly. Makeup could only hide so much. And the eyes often gave away more than what the mouth wanted to tell, but I stuffed the pain anyway. I would be okay, as long as no one asked me how I was.

I learned to try and focus on the things that made me smile. Laugh even. Even if it wasn't for long. Slowly, I acknowledged that there would never be any flowers or chocolates. Compromising myself hadn't yielded what I expected, and I struggled to embrace the woman that stood in front of me. I desperately wanted to paint the picture that I was with a man who wanted to be with me, but it wasn't for the reasons that I wanted.

They say that the truth sets you free, but it can also be hard, and as much as I struggled with it, I still allowed myself to believe that I could change a situation that did not want to be changed. And although I watched the misdemeanours like I was watching a movie on the screen, I couldn't get far away enough from the reality that I was the woman playing the leading role. There were days that I lifted my head far enough to face the stark reality of where I was, but I remained for longer than I believed I would. Sometimes, I was held by the enticement of words. At other times, I felt I lacked the resolve to walk away or entrapped by a dark cloud that had swallowed me.

I don't remember details of the first violation—where it occurred or when—but that may be because life has a way of healing with space and time. I'm not sure if it was during this time that I learned to become my greatest enemy. My words started to berate me with my days increasingly becoming imprisoned in a vault of hopelessness, waiting for someone to set me free.

I became accustomed to sitting at the back of the church on the Sundays that I attended, out of fear of drawing too much attention to myself. Work proved more difficult, with the lie of being overweight less convincing; overeating wouldn't generate weight gain within a short period. Amidst the turmoil that had befriended me, judgement was constantly looming alongside the fear of the truth being leaked out. I knew that what I was about to do was wrong, and guilt gorged itself within me, but the thought of carrying his child weighted more. I had frequented certain streets with him whilst he had acknowledged several women with children that he claimed were his.

I can't remember if I ever told him. I know that I ignored his phone calls and his visits to my house for some time, but I don't know how long this was for or what led me to start speaking to him again. But time would tell.

I had gone to his house to get the money that belonged to me. He told me that he had sold my car and stressed that I would have to come for it if I wanted the money. When I arrived, he told me he had hidden it under the floorboards. The more I impressed, the more obvious it became that he had no intention of releasing it to me. He had already stripped layers from me, which echoed that I had no value. Even when confronted with the lie he had led me to believe, he acted as if it was nothing, inviting me to search for the money myself. I was hesitant, but I proceeded to look anyway. From the words exchanged, I knew that any money I found would not leave the property with me. His eyes held onto me, and perhaps, tired of my charade, he reached for me, and I knew that I was locked in a place that had been familiar. I wrestled and managed to loosen myself, only for him to secure a tighter grip. I called for him to release me, smattered with the words 'no', feeling the loss of power with each move.

Thoughts shrouded my mind that he would overpower me, but I told myself that I just needed to inflict enough pain, causing him to relent or at least create an opportunity for me to escape. I resisted sharply, using the force of my body, but it was only enough for him to curse and relinquish his captor again. As his weight pressed against me, I continued to fight, but I saw that this heightened the experience for him. I surrendered and laid still, with my mind trying to find something that could distance me as far as possible. I noticed the movements of his body change as if the pleasure diminished to some degree. I don't know if he momentarily became aware of what was happening, but I heard the loud kissing of his teeth.

Going through the first abortion had rendered enough turmoil, and yet, here I was again. I had taken the morning-after pill so many times that it seemed that my body had given up responding to them. I resolved not to return to a community hospital, afraid I might see someone I knew or have the abortion traced to me. Yet again, I had to go back to God and ask for His forgiveness.

Whilst the silence protected me, it felt as if it was slowly drawing my breath away. I had navigated through one abortion, and I now had to muster the strength to do it again. The loss of a child permeated my thinking, and although God would not hold this against me, I knew this wasn't where I dreamed I would be. Thoughts of giving birth to a child I would have to give an answer to about the conception sickened me, and I couldn't entertain him coming around me exercising his rights to see the child. Nor did I want to walk the streets colliding with other children who were half-siblings unbeknown to me. But no matter how much misery and pain I had endured, I had not been engulfed by it all despite coming so close.

I refused his efforts to contact me, and his arrival at the door of my family home did not persuade me. Certain family members knew the story in part, and I had deliberately kept it this way. Had they not urged me to talk to him, I am not confident that I would have done so. It had been weeks since I had seen or spoken with him, and I wasn't sure how I would feel seeing him again. My family had been instructed that I would be opposite the house and to come for me had I not returned after a specific period of time. I agreed that I needed closure and that it was only right that he knew what had happened to his child. Having told him, I remember him lowering his head to the steering wheel, followed by the heavy pounding of fists which surprised me. He asked me why I didn't tell him before going ahead with the abortion. I reminded him of what he did and made it clear that I had begun living my life without him. I suggested that he did the same.

A New Chapter

Although this chapter of my life had ended, I still walked with pain and guilt. I don't even know how I managed to walk down the hill to enter the building or squeeze through the doors as I waited for condemnation to greet me. I sat uncomfortably through the service, waiting for it to pounce, but it never came. At the end of service, I breezed past people, shaking hands whilst holding limiting conversations. I believe that one of the prominent women in the church who was well known to me had been watching me, and somehow, my eyes met hers. Don't ask me how, but I knew that she knew. Standing in front of her, she reached for my hands and held them firmly, but gently, and I knew that I couldn't release myself. She started to cry and proceeded to just hold me. No words were exchanged, neither were they necessary. The tears gushed from within me as if everything I was holding onto was given the keys to freedom. I'm not sure if I'd ever felt love the way I did this particular Sunday. She prayed for me before we separated.

That was over twenty years ago, and I have never forgotten how God extended His love towards me. I was expecting to be embarrassed, but I learned a valuable lesson that day, simply that God is a God of love, no matter how far we go.

It was years later before I saw him again. The first was on public transport where he came and sat beside me. I had seen him from the window, waiting to embark and knew that if I attempted to get off, our paths would still have crossed. I had prayed for forgiveness, and I guess that this was the true test that I no longer held these acts against him. I saw him again whilst out shopping. He was accompanied by a woman and children. Although we were inches apart and walking in the opposite direction, I am not certain if he saw me. I did not acknowledge him, neither did he acknowledge me.

Although this is my story, I know that countless women have similar stories too. I also know that just as God reached for me and extended His arms towards me in my moments of pain, He will do the same for someone else. Just as God was waiting to show His love for me, I know that He wants to show how much He loves you too.

14

A LIFE WELL LIVED: NAVIGATING LIFE THE TRINIDADIAN WAY

BERYL RENAUD-BREWSTER

My name is Beryl Irma Renaud-Brewster. I am a mother, a grandmother, a retired nurse, a registered nurse teacher, and proud to be a Trinidadian. I am also the widow of an intelligent, humorous, and loving man to whom I was married for 63 years. I am pleased with my life. I have crossed over and under the River Thames. I have seen my children, grandchildren, and great-grand-children grow and achieve. I have milked a cow and knitted socks for World War II soldiers. I have nursed patients, taught in primary, secondary, and tertiary insti-tutions, and I secretly married the man I love. I have experienced Commonwealth Day celebrations in the presence of members of the U.K. Royal Family. I received a National Award—The Public Service Medal of Merit (Gold)—recognising my outstanding service to Trinidad and Tobago in the sphere of Public Health. I have sung, laughed, cried, rebelled, resisted, and stood up for my beliefs.

Now, at 84, I find myself navigating one of the most challenging periods of my life. I have nothing to do!

I come from a family where people live a long time—a blessing I am sure, but I struggle to see how I might fill the next few years. In the meantime, while I still have my wits about me, I finally agreed to get my story written down for my family.

My story is one of independence, ambition, and resilience, set against a backdrop of Trinidadian colonialism, and later, a newly independent society.

Life will present challenges and difficulties for every one of us, but I believe that we all can do well. Most things are possible with guidance and encouragement. I pray that you might find one or both here as you read about my experiences.

I was born in San Fernando Colonial Hospital, Trinidad, on August 1st, 1936. The fourth child of eight. When I was 18 months old, my father became terribly ill, leaving my mother to care for four children and a newborn baby—my little sister. As a result, I went to live with Tantie (Aunty) until I was three years old.

I enjoyed my childhood. I was a lively girl who played a lot and often got into a mess. Games like 'Jane and Louisa will soon come home', hopscotch, and rounders were some of my favourites.

My family was pious—we were Seventh Day Adventists. I grew up in the church and played the organ. My parents founded the Seventh Day Adventist Church in Point

Fortin. They trained the choir and held cantatas to raise funds for a church building. I remember starting a concert with my opening speech when I was about three years old:

"Violets sweet violets. Only a penny sweet violets. Molly's little hands were blue with the cold as she held out her fragment flowers beseechingly." Then, the choir sang.

Every morning, before Daddy went to work, and every evening, we had family worship. During evening worship, we had to resolve any misunderstandings that occurred during the day. Our parents made us say sorry to each other. This probably explains the loving relationship that now exists among us as adults.

Trinidad imported some of the Victorian values and legal systems that lingered in British society. Mother was very prim and proper. Daddy was proper too, but he was also a very loving and kind gentleman. Conservative values were particularly prevalent with regards to societal beliefs and practices surrounding the family. There was a great shame in having children out of wedlock, and it was not uncommon for children to be taken from unmarried mothers and placed with married couples.

Mother always told us that we had an older brother called Hugh who lived with her aunt.

When I was six years old, I was taken to the San Fernando Colonial Hospital with a sore throat. On the way to the ward, Mother saw a young man leaving the hospital, and she stopped him.

"Do you know who I am?" she asked.

"No, but you look like people I know."

"I am your mother."

And so it was that I met my brother. At the time, he was a young pharmacy student. I remember his shock once given that information. After that, he came to look for me every day in the hospital. He would ask me the names of my brothers and sisters. I always named them in order, starting with him. He knew that we knew about him. He was never left out. He became a major part of the family and is now in our regular monthly family chat.

When I was 16, my eldest sister had a baby. One day, we were at home, and she asked for someone to fetch her some water. I was washing dishes at the time, so I asked my little brother to get it. He didn't. My sister got upset, and Mother thought that I ignored her because I looked down upon her for having a baby out of wedlock. She was wrong—I loved the little baby. Mother went outside to get a whip. When I saw her coming, I dropped the plates with a resounding crash. She changed her mind and went away with her whip.

Nobody could hit me and get away with it. One time, a girl hit me, so I ran her all the way home, past her mummy's porch, under her mother's bed and hit her back. As a four-year-old living with Tantie, I bit a church brother's thumb as he was trying to get me to visit my sick mother, who I thought was very strict and scary. Some say I was naughty—a little terror. I don't think this was the case at all. I simply stood up for what I believed was right.

Married Life

When I was 20, I met a man that did the same. I met Vernon, my husband-to-be, at work. We both taught at the same school, Guapo Government Primary School. I started there in April 1956. One day in September, I saw Vernon in the hallway talking to another female teacher. He teasingly complained to me:

"Miss, is Wednesday and I ain't get a letter yet?"

I told my sisters of this encounter when I got home, and they said that I should not let an opportunity like that pass. So, though he was teasing, I wrote him a letter about giving himself to the Lord. I posted it to the school, but he never mentioned receiving it. A few days later, I received a response in which he expressed his interest in me. We began talking to each other more frequently, and we became friends. About five months later, he came home to meet my parents. Mother said to him, *"I was expecting you"*. Apparently, I talked about him a lot.

My family disapproved of him. When my mother first met Mr Brewster, she did not like him. One of the first things she said was that he walked as if he was 'chipping' behind a steel band. I don't know how much you know about steel bands, but they had a very grass-root origin. For the aspirational, anyone interested in steel pans was considered something of a ruffian. Despite limited opportunities, my mother had high ambitions for all of her children, and as far as she was concerned, he was not what she wanted for her daughter.

Nevertheless, I liked him. He was popular and rebellious but in a principled way. He did not have blind respect for authority, and he would not do things that went against his morals. He would not run his classes differently for the sake of inspectors. He was sent from a city school to my school in the country as punishment after disobeying the Principal.

He had grown up as a Jehovah Witness, but I made it clear I would not marry someone who was not a Seventh Day Adventist. He converted and got baptised.

If you wished to marry in Trinidad, you had to post banns in the Warden's Office, referred to today as the Ministry of Finance. It costs $1.20, and the notice would be posted for everyone to view. Vernon went to the Warden's Office to determine what kind of questions they would ask and posted the banns. Someone saw our notice and told my sister, who told Mother, and she went to the office and told them to take it down. We then posted a second notice in La Brea, where it was less likely to be seen and opposed by anyone we knew. In those days, if you were under 21, you needed your father's consent to marry. A man in the Warden's Office asked if Mr Renaud was my father as we resembled one another. I said yes. The gentleman used to take payslips from Daddy for processing. The enquiring gentleman said, *"Your father is a nice man. He won't mind you being married."* So, without our asking, he filled out and signed the consent form on Daddy's behalf. We waited a while to see if anybody would find out; three months passed, and nobody mentioned a thing, and so we assumed that they did not know.

School ended on Friday, and we married on the following Monday. Vernon's brother was my witness—that was my first time meeting him. On my side, Tantie's friend went with me. Although this was one of the biggest conflicts I have had to navigate, I have no regrets. If I had to go back, I would do it again. I was blessed with a husband who was loving, encouraging and hard-working, and that mattered more than any preconceived misconceptions or plans for my life anyone might have had.

Indeed, my choice of husband was fundamental in shaping how I was able to navigate the other big challenge I encountered in my life's journey—the balancing of a career and motherhood.

Life In The UK

Opportunities and career options were limited for Black Trinidadians. These limits were further compounded by colourism, with certain privileges and comparatively better treatment extended to Black people of lighter complexion. Some jobs, such as working in banks, were only open to people of lighter colour. Having a light complexion meant I could evade the brunt of racial prejudice on Trinidadian soil, though it did not protect me much once I reached the UK.

I always wanted to be a nurse, but I came from a family of teachers. My mother was one of the first Black women to become a teacher, and she wanted all her children to become teachers. Therefore, we all started our careers with teaching. Some of us stuck to teaching, while others transitioned into various careers later on. All of us pursued caring professions. After teaching in Guapo for three years, I noticed a report in the newspaper of a lady who had just come back from nursing in England and was sharing her experience. I wrote to her hospital, and in a short time, I was interviewed by the British Council and accepted. I arrived in England on December 13th, 1958 and started working at St. Mary's Hospital, Plaistow, on January 1st, 1959.

Before arriving, I thought England was an exceptional place where people knew how to behave and speak properly. I soon found out that was not true. I came from the Trinidadian aspiring classes and encountered the English working class. My understanding of what it meant to be English had been informed by propaganda framed around the lives and experiences of the middle and upper classes. In contrast, I was confronted with people who did not bathe every day because they could not afford the heating.

When I started nursing, I realised that my husband had type 1 diabetes, so I got him started on treatment. We had been married for five years and had no babies. After treatment began, two of our three children came in quick succession. The first, my baby girl Perle, was born in 1961, followed by her little brother Jerry eleven months later.

Myrna was born in 1964. People often say that a woman must choose between a career or motherhood—she cannot do both. That was not my story; I remained a nurse and combined my work experiences to qualify as a registered nurse teacher in 1990. I pursued further education, and in 1983, I completed my bachelor's degree in Social Science and History at the University of the West Indies (UWI) in St Augustine. Next came my postgraduate diploma in Public Administration in 1990 (also from UWI St Augustine), and I received my masters in Sociology from the London School of Economics and Political Science while working at the Royal College of Nursing in 1994.

That said, doing both was challenging. Life began to change once we became working parents. I used to do night duty so that Vernon would care for the children in the night, and I would look after them in the day. Perle would cry and fall asleep by the door after Vernon left for work. Eventually, we took Perle and Jerry to a childminder. On an impromptu visit, I discovered my babies blue as she had turned off the heating during a particularly bad winter in 1963. Mother (who had begun writing to me once I came to England) said that I should bring them home and she would take care of them.

Perle was 22 months, her brother 11 months. When I arrived back in Trinidad, I stayed a few months, working at Trinidad Community Hospital to give my children time to adjust before my return to England. They stayed with my mother for five years. They were spoiled dearly. While away, I missed Perle. I knew that Mother loved boys, so I did not worry for him, but I wasn't sure how my daughter would be getting on. Perle reports that Mother was protective towards Jerry, and so he was never told off. Perle, as a consequence, connived to always have him take the blame so she wouldn't get into trouble. I next saw them in 1968. On returning to Trinidad, I worked as a Health Visitor and went back to England to do short courses. In 1973, I spent a year in Jamaica studying Nurse Management on a government scholarship. When I was away for study, the children stayed with their father. He encouraged me to make use of the opportunities presented even when I was unsure about leaving. I wish to recognise his contribution as a founding member of Lifeline, its first Chairman, and as Director of the Students Advisory Service, University of the West Indies (UWI), St. Augustine Trinidad.

I do not have any regrets about the decision to leave my children with my mother. Nevertheless, it was difficult! Many times, I wanted to go back and get my children. Being away from them affected our bond, especially with my son. When I came back, Perle did not like me much. In her eyes, I was old and had too many rules. My mother was not the strict disciplinarian for her grand-children as she had been with her children, and Daddy was a big softie as a grandfather. Perle says that all of a sudden, I showed up with rules and discipline, rationed cookies and sweets, and gave instructions about how to position the soup bowl. Under my care, Perle could clean a house at 11. As she grew older and settled down, she realised what it was like to be a woman and had more sympathy for my parenting. Until then, it was a misery.

When I first met Perle after our time apart, I thought she was loud and did not know how to behave. Of course, my own mother would have said the same thing about me. According to her account, going on holiday to their grandma's house was like escaping prison and going back to normal. I was not strict, she says, her Daddy was. I was a pain. All I know is that I learned from my mother's training during my own upbringing that children had to behave properly.

Although it was challenging, I learned from my mothering experience while working that it can be done. I would not encourage any young person to think they cannot have a career while being a parent. I would not let them entertain such an idea. I had live-in help to take care of the domestic chores. I always had this, from the time I arrived from England. I was able to afford it because my husband and I both worked. I also made parenting a priority—simply having the means is not enough. When something is a priority, you find the means to make it happen, and so I intentionally put things in place financially and made sacrifices elsewhere. With proper organising and support, parenting while working can be done.

It is now 2021, and I am retired from my responsibilities as mother, wife, nurse, and teacher. I am now Beryl. Easy-going, no fuss Beryl. A woman who puts her best foot forward in all she did. I like people, and I hope people remember me as liking them. I want people to under-stand and believe that success is possible if you seek guidance. It doesn't always happen in a day, but it can happen with determination, support, and discipline. I did not go out searching for opportunities, but I have always made use of those that have come my way. I believe in a superior power and know that I have been blessed.

Embrace life, say yes, and do good to others.

15

NO LOST CAUSES: NAVIGATING TEENAGE MOTHERHOOD

PATSY GRANT

It was a Saturday morning in the city of Liverpool, and the excitement I felt at the thought of going to my elder sister's house made me happy. Saturday was the only day that I could leave the house without my parents. During the week, I was only allowed to go to school and return home. My evenings were for homework and assisting my mother in the kitchen. I was to make sure I did my chores at home and run errands for my mum.

Our house was a five-bedroom house, with a front room, a living room, and a dining room. I executed my plan perfectly by starting my chores early in the morning. I needed to finish my tasks early in the day; otherwise, I risked jeopardising my chance of going to my sister's house. If I left late, I'd have to go to Aunt Sybil's house with mum, so I could not take any chances.

I had only two weeks of school left before the start of the six-week school holidays, and I was determined to enjoy it. I finished my chores and mum was happy. My father was indifferent; all he was interested in was his horses.

I was the only sibling left at home; I am the youngest child of seven. Everyone at that time had left home to make a life for themselves. I was a daddy's girl, and he expected so much of me. He spoilt me by giving me everything I asked for. Every school trip abroad, I was on it; he would also buy me the latest bicycles. I have two older sisters who I looked up to; they both had teenage pregnancies. That's why my father was lenient with me, as he didn't want me to make the same mistake.

I couldn't wait to put my new clothes on. I loved to dress up; I was quite a trendy teenager. I had a brand-new lemon-coloured dress and a pair of roman sandals with lemon-coloured laces tied up to my knees. As a fifteen-year-old, I was not allowed to wear makeup, only eyeliner and lip gloss. As I stepped out, I could smell the fragrance of geranium plants in the garden. I looked up at the blue sky and sunshine; the temperature was perfect.

As I started walking, I heard the voice of my mother echoing down the street: *"Make sure you are in by 10.00 p.m."* My usual time for return was 8 p.m. during school term, but for some reason, she allotted me an extra two hours. I think it was because I was going to my sister's house. I was so excited to go to a place where I could be free, and my sister was not too strict. Thank God.

My mother had given me five pounds to spend; I was in my element. I looked good in my new dress and new sandals. It was unusual for mum to let me wear fashion because she was a seamstress; she made my clothes herself. Mum made me choose from patterns; she bought in John Lewis. So, you can imagine how I felt on this particular day. I was elated.

As I walked down my sister's street, I could see my little niece eagerly waiting for me to arrive. She was so excited, and the feeling was mutual. I helped my sister clean her home, and later in the day, we sat down to eat dinner together. As we ate, I casually mentioned a youth club I had heard about in school where all my friends and a couple of my cousins frequented. My sister could see the direction my conversation was going, and before I could ask, she permitted me to go.

Julian

I had never been to the Methodist youth club before; this was my first experience as a teenager going out amongst my peers. I met my two cousins inside, and they were so happy to see me. The music was loud, and the bass sounded like a thunder roll, but I was used to it because my brother, Tony, had a sound system called the Mighty Beast.

Tony used to play the sound system at home when our parents worked the night shift.

The hall was thick with ganja smoke, and the sound of reggae echoed through the walls. Men and women slow jammed to the reggae beat, gyrating bodies of men and women were moving in sync with each other. I liked what I saw.

I stood aside, swaying to the reggae beat when I felt someone's touch. I ignored it at first; I didn't even bother to look around. This person was persistent and tugged at my hand, this time, indicating that he wanted to dance with me. I hesitated, but when I looked into his face, I saw the most handsome boy in the whole building, and he was asking me for a dance. We danced together all evening until it was time to leave. He offered to escort me back to my sister's house. I collected my coat from the cloakroom, said goodbye to my cousins, and left with my newfound friend.

His name was Julian; he was nothing like the boys at school. He appeared to be more mature than they were. I liked everything about him. We talked about family, school, and the things we loved to do outside of school.

I arrived at my sister's at 9.30 p.m. My sister told me to make my way to Aunt Sybils to meet my mum. That was another half an hour's walk, but I was willing because it meant I could spend a bit more time with Julian.

I was 15 minutes late, but I didn't care. Julian and I exchanged phone numbers and agreed to meet the following Saturday. We spoke every day on the phone, and we came to a decision. We couldn't wait until Saturday to see each other, so we arranged to meet after school. He met me every day at school until school broke up for the six-week school holidays. We walked through the park every day along with my cousins, as they went to the same school as I did. Our relationship transitioned from being friends to becoming an item; we were now officially boyfriend and girlfriend.

I never had a boyfriend before; he was my first, and I was his. Neither one of us had experienced a sexual encounter before, but all that was about to change.

My parents worked night shifts; my mum worked permanent nights, and my dad worked nights two weeks on and two weeks off. So, it was easy to plan when we were going to spend time together.

One particular week, when both my parents were away doing the night shift, I planned for Julian to visit. I had butterflies in my stomach; this was the first time I had ever brought a boy to my parents' house.

He was punctual; I was impressed, excited, but mostly anxious. I remember babysitting my little niece at the time. As soon as Julian arrived, I put her to bed so we could be alone. I connected my brother's sound system; the music played softly, and we began dancing and kissing, and one thing led to another, and that was it; we were no longer virgins.

My life changed from that day; what took place that night was now a regular occurrence. We were deeply in love; at least, I thought that's what it was. We were inseparable. My mum welcomed Julian, but my dad wasn't as accommodating as she was. My dad banned him from coming into our house but allowed him to stand outside. I think this was because he had dreadlocks. He naturally assumed he smoked weed. He wasn't wrong; I had also started to smoke weed.

I introduced him to my eldest sister, and it happened that his sister, Christine, was also a good friend of hers. Julian's mother welcomed me into her home with open arms. She lived about five minutes away from my sister, so now I had an excuse to go to my sister's house.

We had been together for almost a year. Our relationship was solid. The school summer holidays were in a couple of months, and I was revising for my mock exams. I was an A+ student in all subjects; that's why my father kept a close eye on me because he didn't want the same fate to happen to me like my sisters.

My dad continued to give me a hard time because of Julian. I couldn't understand why because my sister's boyfriend was also a Rasta. Even after a year, he would not allow him into our home, and although my mum loved him, she was powerless and could not go against my father's word. His famous words were, 'Not under my roof'. As time went on, I began to resent my father and his behaviour towards Julian. So, I started coming in late from school. I lost interest in my schoolwork, and my grades nosedived.

During the six weeks holiday, Julian and I eloped to London for a few weeks. We stayed with my other sister and her friends. We enjoyed our time together in London, especially at Notting Hill carnival. We were free to do as we liked; I suppose we were like grown-ups. I took the child benefit book with me to finance ourselves.

I knew my dad was distraught and angry with us. I was scared to go home, but I had no choice because school was about to resume, and the worst thing was, my school was reopening on my birthday. Julian's mum was a lot more understanding and approachable. She even sent us money to buy food which was a great help as we ran out of food a few times.

I sat on the National Express Coach, terrified at the thought of going home, worried about what my father would say or do. I knew he worked the night shift, so I thought if I could arrive home and change into my uniform and leave for school before he got in, I could avoid any confrontation.

When I arrived home, I was relieved he wasn't there, but then I heard the keys turn in the lock. I thought that's it; I'm dead now. Mum is not even home from work yet to save me, but instead, he looked happy to see me. I was surprised. He asked if I just arrived home. I answered yes, but I was still scared he might hit me, but surprisingly, he said I should hurry up so I wouldn't be late for school.

Motherhood

The next few months were a strain between dad and me. His disliking for Julian grew worse. It was unbearable; Julian was the love of my life. I'd do anything to see him. I started to stay out all night at his house; his mum would not know I was there at times.

In November, Julian's mother took a vacation to Dominica. I stayed at his house almost every night while she was away. I still attended school, but I skipped lessons on a few occasions or skipped the whole day here and there. As time went on, I began to sense changes in my body; my breasts felt tender, and when I missed my period, I started to worry. Julian bought me a pregnancy test, and when the result came back positive, I was speechless. I cried for the whole day. I refused to believe it, so I called my GP. I made an appointment for the next day.

As I entered the doctor's surgery, my heart began to palpate. I was thinking about what my parents' reaction would be if I were pregnant. I was not even sure if the doctors would tell my parents I had come for the pregnancy test. They took a blood test from me and told me to call them the next day. I was anxious. However, I called the doctors from the phone box, and they gave me the result of the pregnancy test. It was positive.

Our whole lives changed from that moment because we decided we were going to keep our baby. We thought it would stop my father constantly trying to split us up. That was our immature way of thinking anyway.

We were both sixteen years old; I guess we were children having a child.

My parents knew nothing; I was too scared to tell them, so I attended my first hospital appointment alone. I was so afraid.

I continued to go to school, as usual; no one suspected a thing. I hid my morning sickness at home from my parents and my teachers at school. One day, I came home from school earlier than usual as I was not feeling very well. I walked into the living room and saw an opened letter standing tall on the mantlepiece. On the note, it read Liverpool Maternity Hospital. I knew it was my letter; I ran upstairs to my room. My father had opened the letter because he thought it belonged to him as we share the same initials, and the letter did not indicate whether it was for a Mr. or Miss. He asked me if the letter belonged to me, and I replied yes. He huffed, and that was the only thing he said to me for the whole nine months. My mum and dad were so disappointed in me. I had let them down just like my other two sisters.

I continued to go to school until I was four months pregnant. It was hard because I was always tired, not to mention I was having morning sickness in my exams. As my pregnancy began to show, my mother made me a couple of navy-blue smock dresses to hide my bump. Still, my teacher thought otherwise and said it was a distraction to the rest of the school, so my teacher advised my parents to send me to the school for pregnant schoolgirls. The teachers there were very supportive, and it was there that I passed all my exams with good grades. If I had not transferred to that school, my grades would not have been as good as they were.

I had tremendous support from family members throughout my pregnancy, especially my mum, Julian's mum, my sister Marcia, and Julian's two sisters—Geraldine and Christine. My Aunt Sybil knitted yellow and white baby cardigans for me. I didn't want for anything. I had everything a newborn baby needed. The only thing I wanted now was for my dad to talk to me. I knew he was still upset with me. I heard my mum and dad saying that my life was finished and there was no hope for me. I laid on my bed crying; I had returned home now, safe with my parents, but my dad still would not talk to me.

One night, when my mum was at work on her usual night shift. I had felt pain throughout the night. I knew I was in labour, but I was too embarrassed to tell my dad, so I held out until the morning. As soon as I heard the key turn in the door, I held my stomach and moved towards the top of the stairs. My mom looked up at me, and my waters broke at the same time.

The ambulance took me to the hospital, where I remained in labour for twelve hours. Julian met me there. I was about to become a mum, and my life would change forever after that.

My baby daughter was born, and Julian and I were ecstatic. Everyone came to visit, and only one person was missing—my dad.

It was a requirement for all first-time mothers to remain in the hospital for seven days. On my fourth day, which was a Sunday, my dad came to visit, and he brought me Sunday dinner. I saw the look on his face, and I put his granddaughter into his arms. I believe this was the turning point in my father's relationship with me.

I was discharged home from the hospital the following week. It was so good to be home. I went upstairs to my room, only to find my dad had redecorated and changed the carpet in my room. He even changed his attitude toward Julian; they became best friends from that day forward.

Julian and I left Liverpool with our five-month-old baby daughter, Charlene, to start a new life in London with Julian's sister, Christine. It was challenging, and we went through a lot, but we had to make it work for our daughter's sake.

Julian and I eventually split up, not because we didn't get on well together, but because he didn't want to live in London, and I was adamant I was not going back to Liverpool. However, life went on. I qualified as a registered nurse, and I am currently a Sister in my department, working for the NHS.

Charlene went on to university to study fine art and textile design. Charlene also formed a singing group called Soultre, which appeared on a UK talent show called X-factor. She was also part of the London Community Gospel Choir. She is a youth mentor to troubled teenagers, and she recently hosted her online talk show, which is just a few of the things she has done.

Although our start in life didn't look promising, we made it work by the grace of God. Mothers, fathers, grandfathers and grandmothers, my word to you is to not give up on your sons and daughters, no matter how far left they have gone. Encourage them even when it looks like there is no hope. Our God is not a God of abandoned projects.

16

DEBT OF SHAME TO DEBT OF GRATITUDE: NAVIGATING DIFFICULT CONVERSATIONS

GANS OWOLABI

My parents came to England in the late 1950s. Both of my parents are Nigerians but have two different faith backgrounds. My mother was raised a Christian, and my dad a Muslim. They got together amidst a lot of objections from both sides of their families and friends.

From a young age, our parents gave us the option to choose which faith we wanted to follow. The only thing they stipulated was they wanted us to believe in God, pray, and give to charity.

My mother had two daughters before she met and married my dad (another reason daddy's friends objected to the marriage). My parents had four children together, three daughters and one son, but my dad always treated my sisters as his own children.

I have been through my fair share of heartache, but I didn't know what pain was until I heard that my mother had died. I had lost one of my sisters the year before, and that devastated me but couldn't compare to how bereft I felt when mummy died.

I remember it clearly as if it were yesterday. I remember smiling as I called my brother when I saw his missed calls. Then he told me mummy had died. I just screamed; I couldn't control it. Everything was hazy. I remember my boss came into the office; he was in the corridor and heard me scream, and somehow, he knew.

I thought it wasn't possible for mummy to have died. I had only seen her the night before, and she was fine. She didn't look sick. I had dropped off the laundry before work, given her a kiss, and told her I would see her after work. She didn't say anything, just gave me a beautiful smile.

Siblings

My parents came from families that quarrelled a lot, and one of the things that they instilled in us was to support each other. My dad would not let us hold an argument for more than a day. If we argued, he would call us together the next day and ask us to resolve it with him as a referee.

When mummy died, my siblings and I supported daddy. My older sister lived in Ireland, and my younger sister was in Yorkshire. Both would come to London to visit every three to six months, so only my brother and I lived in London.

My brother asked my son to move in with daddy, so he would not be alone. My son has sickle cell disease and had his own flat. My brother explained to his nephew that he would have a home for life if he moved in with daddy and would not have to pay for anything. My son, since he was six months old, was in and out of the hospital with many painful sickle crises. So, this proposal seemed like a great solution as they would be able to support each other.

In 2011, my dad was diagnosed with dementia. I'm not sure how I missed it. I had started a new job in 2010 after going through a divorce and redundancy.

It wasn't until my dad had a fire, which started because my dad thought he still had his old gas kettle, and he placed his new electric kettle (that looked like the old one) on the stove. This is when it hit me that something was seriously wrong, so I sought medical help.

After the fire, my dad moved into my home with me. My son stayed with his partner, whilst the insurance company repaired the damage to my dad's home. As the only female family member close by, I automatically became daddy's carer and would liaise with social services to organise carers to come in whilst I was working to assist daddy. Daddy lived with us for eight months and only moved back to his house when my kitchen was being remodelled.

Debts

Other things started to make sense, one being daddy used to go to the bank monthly to collect his pension, but on three occasions, he would reach home, and the money was missing. He usually withdrew between £600-£800. I used to take time off to take him to the bank, but I was contracting, and it meant that I lost out on a day's wages, so I asked my brother to arrange to get authorisation so he could withdraw cash on daddy's behalf.

I trusted my brother with this responsibility, and he gave me no reason not to. I also didn't want this responsibility, especially as my dad had allowed me to use his credit card to buy food and pay my rent and bills. I remember paying it off and then using it again. I remember when things got so heavy because I only made minimum payments, and I went from owing a few hundred pounds to owing thousands of pounds on daddy's credit card.

I remember hiding the letters until one day, my brother found out, and we worked out a way for me to make more than the minimum amount, but the interest still piled up. I asked my brother to contact the bank, request they freeze the interest as daddy had dementia, but he said "no".

I felt so much shame that I had caused this debt. My dad was a man who didn't do debt, who lived within his means and who trusted me. I had told him every time I used the card. I never thought that being made redundant and earning less money would put me in this position. I was disgusted with myself for not managing his money better. I was always playing catch up, robbing Peter to pay Paul. My brother helped me out a couple of times, and I will always be grateful for this as I was desperate. These were my mistakes, and the decisions I made affected my dad's credit.

When my eldest daughter turned 16, we were clashing about everything, and I was the mum who couldn't understand why she wanted to argue with everything I said. Trying to cope with the arguments, issues with my bosses at work, and looking after my youngest daughter who was six, were just too much.

She moved in with daddy while she attended college, which made life easier for everyone. Her brother made sure he kept an eye on her.

Dad

Before my dad died, daddy's carer and I noticed that he wasn't well. I thought he might have a urine infection, and I asked them to check his urine, but they couldn't get a sample, so they sent him home and asked me to collect a sample. I was unable to do this, so I took daddy back to the hospital a couple more times. I remember saying I cannot get a sample and asked if it could be done via a blood test, and they said no. By the third occasion of me taking daddy to the hospital, the doctor on call asked for a bag to be put on daddy, and when they collected a sample, the results showed that daddy had an infection and it had gone to his kidneys. I couldn't believe it. Firstly, why had they not done this before? My dad was in the hospital for eight days before he died. I stayed with him every day. When the doctors indicated on the 7th of June 2016 that they didn't think he would make it through to the next day, I stayed at the hospital. I didn't want to leave him alone or trust that they would fight to save him as I would. I believe he was waiting for my sisters to arrive before he died. When we were all there together, he was so happy, and I thought that he would survive even though the doctors kept saying we should prepare ourselves.

When my dad died, I was distraught. I had been cooking and cleaning and generally keeping him company along with my children. He was such a good role model. He was a man that worked hard, looked after his wife and children, helped countless family and friends along with my mum's transition from Nigeria to England. He helped to counsel couples and families. He wasn't what most people would call a cool dad in so much as he didn't play football with us, but he did have lots of conversations with us (and as it turns out, that is one of the best parts, so you know that he was cool). On Saturdays, we would all watch TV together as a family, and he would ask us about our week. Daddy always started the talk about one thing, e.g., a program on TV, but it would always end up being about education. Our parents encouraged us to study hard and have big aspirations, and dream big.

Family Home

When daddy died, I remember my ex-partner saying that when my brother goes to look for the will, I should go with him. There was an implication there, but I brushed it off. I trusted my brother.

A week after my dad died, my brother announced that he couldn't locate my dad's will, and he was going to sell the flat. I couldn't believe it, and I told him that he knew that daddy didn't want to sell this flat. I reminded him that dad bought it with the sole purpose in mind that it was a base for all of us, and that if for any reason any of us didn't have a place to stay, we could always live there. I couldn't change his mind; I remember going backwards and forwards discussing the matter. I didn't want to have a massive fallout with my brother. I know my father would not like that. My brother reminded me of the debts I had run up and that this could all be cleared. I remembered the overwhelming shame I felt and how I didn't want anyone outside the family to know. I cannot remember if my sisters knew about the debt, but I knew I didn't want other family members or friends to know that I had run up this debt. I was so angry, but I had to keep silent.

I remember I had booked a holiday for my younger daughter, granddaughter, and myself to go away for ten days. I had done a lot of overtime to pay for this holiday and had found a reasonably priced holiday for the three of us. I was trying so hard to let the girls have a fun time as they were both sad at losing their granddad. I remember receiving a text message from my brother in the last few days of the holiday, advising that he had started the probate process, and I was so upset and angry that he couldn't even give me this holiday without reminding me what he was doing.

All through the probate process, I tried to get my brother to change his mind, but he was adamant that the sale of the house was going through. I remember asking him why, and he would say it's a leasehold property and that he didn't want to have to deal with any leasehold duties that would incur costs. Instead of selling the flat, I suggested that he rent it to my son and then we could put the rent into an account.

That money could be put aside for any payments that needed to be made, and after we've had a substantial amount built up, we could all receive an income from the flat for years to come.

No matter what I said, he would always shut me down. The anger I felt at this time couldn't be measured. I remember talking to my friends about it, and I never mentioned the debt I had run up or the shame over the situation. I would say things like, *"He is greedy; there is no reason to sell our family home". "He does not need the money; he already owns his own home". "He only started helping out with my dad when I asked him to manage my dad's account"*.

By my brother saying that he was selling the house, he was effectively evicting my son and daughter, which meant that they would have to move back home.

A year after my dad died, my brother had the flat on the market and was having people come to view the flat. When a prospective buyer came around, my brother gave my son a month to move out. The only problem was that my son was extremely sick in hospital and was in no condition to pack. I remember going to the flat and picking up my parents' documents, pictures, and anything I could carry, and putting them in a cab and taking them to my house over the month.

Whilst on our summer break, my brother sent me a message saying that my son had to move out of the house by the 31st of August. I would be out of the country at this time, and I asked if it could wait one more day until I got back. My brother just shouted at me and told me that we had had enough time and that the house had been sold and we needed to clear the house. He said that he had someone coming to clear everything out.

I cannot express what it was like to know that my brother, someone I loved so much, could do this to his nephew, who he knew was sick and that stress was a big factor in having a crisis. My brother didn't give me the time to get back and move any of my son's possessions. I only managed to save my mum's sewing machine by asking my son's Godmother to hold onto it until I got home. My son lost everything except for his clothes and pictures. The worst part was to find out that the contracts had, at that time, not been signed and that we had at least a couple more weeks before he needed to leave the premises.

I remember the look on my son's face when I told him that everything was gone. I remember the anger that was in my daughters' faces. I remember the feeling in the pit of my stomach. I remember the shame that I couldn't do anything.

Lessons Learned

I'm in a better place now, although writing about it has been challenging. I feel that the relationship I have with my brother is not as great as my sisters, but I love him. My older sister and I speak weekly, and I look forward to our Saturday night catchups over FaceTime. I love discussing the Bible with them. Before lockdown, both of my sisters visited me, and it was so wonderful just hugging, watching TV, and being together.

I just pray that what has happened to me does not happen to anyone else. I pray that whoever reads this does not let themselves be governed by shame. I pray that people realise there are so many more important things in life than money, and we should all learn to manage it well.

I pray that all families make a will, and it is administered by someone neutral. l pray we don't take it for granted that a good job is for life, and we have backup plans and backup plans for the backup plan.

If there is one thing I know now, it is that we must have those difficult end-of-life conversations with our loved ones while we can. I will be having them often with my children.

Know that only God knows what is around every corner and that they should live life to the fullest. Enjoy every moment, but also plan for the future.

HEALING POEM

Healing arrives in all shapes and forms

Healing doesn't follow the norms

Healing differs from people to people

Healing is accustomed to the many storms

Healing does not discriminate

Healing knows no bounds

Healing is there for every case

There's enough healing to go around

Healing knows no boundaries

Healing is not proud

Healing enters in different ways

Healing enters in with no sound

Healing fights for every case

Healing has your back

Healing comes right on time

Healing covers every track

Healing will restore you to health

and healing will restore your wounds

Healing will heal your state of mind

Healing stabilises your mood

Healing gives you peace

Healing makes you smile

Healing adjusts the negatives

Healing stays for a very long while

Healing is a part of the master plan

Healing is who God is

Healing for mankind is standard

And is a part of God's will.

The Scribe

Yvonne H-Williams (Yvonne Netballer)

IG: @the_netball_scribe

AFTERWORD

At the start of the global pandemic, I had an incredible idea to continue to engage with women on the Navigating Life platform. I got together with a team from ICAN Community Church and started to share some blue sky thinking about what this could potentially mean. We shared ideas and concepts about how we could continue to engage and support women during this particular season. What started out as a 12-week program, turned into a weekly Saturday strength building, mind-stretching, empowering virtual forum, with attendees from across the world.

It was during one of these sessions that I had an idea to create an anthology, I had no idea we could even do this. The drive was to create a space for other women to share stories of how they had navigated a season in their life. I wanted for the women to be in a position to inspire other women. I'm super excited that you have read their contributions.

What next...

I hope by now you are reminded that the messenger makes the message unique and as ambassadors of hope, the women who have written these stories are sharing messages of hope, transformation, determination and sagacity.

Do you have a story of hope? Do you have a story of how you have had to navigate a season in your life? Perhaps it's time to take the first step in increasing your capacity for more and allow others to see the journey, to hear the transformation and to feel the impact of your legacy in the years to come.

NOTES

ABOUT THE AUTHORS

1. Deborah Grant CPA-CGA, CITM, CTG

I am an island girl with a passion for people and helping them to live their best version of themselves. I love seeing others happy and I am in a particularly good place on my own journey to purpose. I want to see others on their journey. My focus is mainly in the area of youth and young adults, where I believe a firm foundation will prepare them for the future.

I started DS Grace Inc in 2018, which is the company that operates "Stanley's Room", a private room rented to visitors to the island under the Airbnb brand. I am an ordained Deacon in the African Methodist Episcopal Zion Church.

LinkedIn:
www.linkedin.com/in/deborahgrantchattelhouseaudiotours

Email: debyagrant@gmail.com

Facebook: www.facebook.com/deborah.thompson.9480

Instagram: @chatbarbados

2. Shevonne Carvey

Psychology graduate Mother of 4 beautiful children. Aspiring educational psychologists. Through my experiences as a child, my passion to understand the mind of children is real. Not only to understand them, but to help them understand themselves and how to accomplish their purpose in this world.

Email: Shevyy27@gmail.com

3. Dr. Carmen C. McPherson

An experienced inspirational educational leader, workshop developer, researcher and problem solver. Currently an Assistant High School Principal in Bridgeport CT, USA., and a self-described edupreneur. Creator of Gye Nyame Educational Services, a company that works with organizations to assess and identify their learning needs.

LinkedIn: www.linkedin.com/in/dr-carmen-c-mcpherson-varner-6b56786/

Website: gnesllc.com

Email: gnesllc.comgnesllc@gmail.com

4. Rev Jassica Castillo-Burley

This year I will have been married to Roy for 25 years and I have a son, Elnathan, who is 13 years old. I was born in Nottingham, studied Chemistry in London, lived and worked most of my married life in Hampshire as an analytical chemist. I gave this up to pursue whatever God had in store for me. I am now a priest in the Church of England, having to return to study but this time in Cambridge. I now live in Shropshire. Beside music, singing and worship my main ministry is pastoral.

Instagram: @Jassica-1

Facebook & LinkedIn: Jassica Castillo-Burley

Email: princessjassica1@googlemail.com

5. Rona Anderson

Happiness Consultant and International Development Partnerships Manager is dedicated to improving the happiness and wellbeing of all those in need; helping to increase performance and productivity. She is passionate about empowering people out of physical, emotional and spiritual poverty. She is also a Community Wellbeing Project Manager, Director of Global Missions, founder of Happiness By Mission, Speaker and Author.

Facebook: www.facebook.com/rona.anderson.585/

Website: www.ronaanderson.com

LinkedIn: www.linkedin.com/in/rona-anderson-590b231b2/

Email: rona@ronaanderson.com

6. Nadine Forde

I am a child of God, servant of the King and worshipper. Blessed with two beautiful daughters. I'm a single mom and survivor. Also a Business owner, Worship leader, prayer intercessor and now Author!! The Lord say He will, *"give me a future and a hope"*, the possibilities are unlimited.

7. Julie Braham

A mother, British born of Jamaican origin. A career in adult nursing that's spans over 30 years. An active member of the Royal College of Nursing. When I'm not working I love nature walks where I get inspired. I have an interest in encouraging people, especially women, I also play an active part in women's ministry in church.

Instagram: @juliebramo

Facebook: Julie Braham

Email: juliebakas@hotmail.com

8. Lara Samuel

I am a wife to Michael Samuel and mother to Hannah, Elizabeth and Jeremiah.

I am the Founder of High Heritage Charity; we work to support young black people in our communities to advance and develop their skills.

I work in the NHS and I also Coach with the John Maxwell Team. I have a passion for the next generation of leaders.

Facebook: @Lara Samuel

Linkedin: Lara Samuel

Email: trueyou20200@yahoo.com

Instagram: @high_heritage_charityDetails....

9. Rhonda Ioniez

'RHONDA IONIEZ' is a Christian mother with two children and has been an employee for the NHS as a neonatal nurse and midwife. Over the years she has worked voluntarily as a Listener Samaritan, serves as a school governor and engages in various community ventures. Her hobbies include travelling, collecting sporting memorabilia and reading.

Email: rhondaioniez21@gmail.com

10. Claudette Samuel

Mother, Grandmother and Foster carer, Aspiring Property & Business Owner, founder member of Savvy Women Investors Academy (SWIA). Semi-retired living her best life in the now, changing the environment around her one encouraging word at a time.

Email: claudettesamuel@yahoo.co.uk

Facebook: Claudette Samuel | Facebook

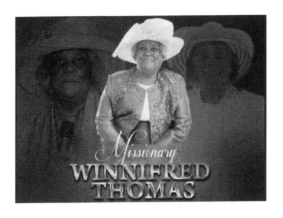

II. Written by Dawn Thomas Wallace (Daughter)

A dynamic woman who lived to serve and raise others to their highest height. Born and raised in Jamaica, Winnifred enjoyed a life of great wealth and luxury. Even so, she desired more than what the fleeting pleasures of riches could offer and unashamedly became a devoted Christian in a hostile world – *"from riches to rags"* for Christ. Winnifred, however, was rich in good works towards the weak, the poor and all who crossed her path.

Winnifred Thomas, correctly described as a Woman of God, Mother in Zion, worshipper, counsellor, defender of the weak, "a proper Jamaican lady". To us: Mum.

Sleep on, Mummy. You have finished your work and earned a crown of righteousness, which God Himself will give you. We are so proud of you.

12. Lilian W Mwangi

A Christian, a wife and a mother of two. She is a trained early years education and special needs practitioner. She loves working with kids. She loves to design and make handmade cards and gifts @lilltastic designs. She lives in United Kingdom with her family.

13. Charlene Brown

I am a poet, author and writer who has facilitated writing for well being workshops, with the purpose of encouraging and inspiring others. I have also encouraged women through public speaking and the written word. I have been involved with empowering women suffering from abuse and young people with addictions.

Email: info@charlenebrown.co.uk

Instagram: @charlene.abrown

Facebook: charlene.brown.397948

LinkedIn: charlene-brown-44722424

14. Beryl Brewster

A retired community health nurse, educator, manager and consultant. She has worked in these areas:

- The Government of Trinidad and Tobago
- The Royal College of Nursing, England
- The Joint Commission International of the United States
- The Registered Nurses Association

She is the widow of Vernon Brewster and the mother of Perle, Jerry and Myrna.

15. Patsy Grant

Born in Liverpool in the sixties to Jamaican parents, the youngest of seven children. She is a qualified nurse and works for NHSBT (blood and transplant). She is the mother of a beautiful daughter called Charlene. She is an ordained minister whom the Lord has called as a Prophetess to the Nations.

Email: patsy.grant.04@gmail.com

Instagram: @patsylovesmelon

Twitter: @patsylovesmelon

16. Ganiat Owolabi

I'm a 56-year-old woman, who's worked in ICT for 20+ years. God blesses me every day and He has given me the connections and the courage to write part of my life journey. Ever since I said Yes to Him, He has increased my Blessings.

ALSO BY CLAUDINE REID MBE

Navigating Life:

Health, Grief & Loss

———————

Navigating Life:

Mindset, Identity & Relationships

———————

ABOUT CLAUDINE REID MBE

Claudine Reid MBE

MY MISSION IS TO CREATE MORE LEADERS

Social entrepreneur, business psychologist, leadership coach, wife and mother. Claudine has more than 20 years of experience co-directing an award-winning, 7 figure social enterprise. Her expertise in growing people's talents, organisational development, and motivating others to develop successful habits make her a unique, passionate and inspirational leader and consultant.

www.claudinereidmbe.com

DIVINE FLOW PUBLISHING

Publishing People of Influence

onto Platforms for Impact.

The Lord gives the word [of power];
the women who bear and publish [the news]
are a great host. Psalm 68:11 AMPC

www.DivineFlowPublishing.com

SOME HELPFUL AGENCY NUMBERS

United Kingdom Emergency Services Number - 999

National Domestic Violence Helpline 0808 2000 247

(24-hour freephone), run by Refuge and Women's Aid.

Refuge: http://www.refuge.org.uk Supports women, children and men with services including refuges.

Women's Aid: http://www.womensaid.org.uk Working to end domestic abuse against women and children.

Samaritans: 116 123 (24 hours) http://www.samaritans.org Someone to listen, whatever people are going through.

Multiple Sclerosis - MS Society https://www.mssociety.org.uk/ Contact: 0808 800 8000

Endometriosis Society https://www.endometriosis-uk.org/ Helpline: 0808 808 2227 Telephone: 020 7222 2781

Christians Against Poverty Contact: 0800 328 0006

https://capuk.org Email: info@capuk.org

The Miscarriage Association

https://www.miscarriageassociation.org.uk/ Contact:01924 200 799 Email: info@miscarriageassociation.org.uk

Outside the UK

In the USA, the Domestic Violence Hotline is

1-800-799-SAFE (7233)

Other international helplines may be found via

http://www.befrienders.org

Printed in Great Britain
by Amazon